The BIG BOOK *of Presidents*

From George Washington to Barack Obama

Sky Pony Press books may be purchased in bulk at special discounts for sales promotion, corporate gifts, fund-raising, or educational purposes. Special editions can also be created to specifications. For details, contact the Special Sales Department, Sky Pony Press, 307 West 36th Street, 11th Floor, New York, NY 10018 or info@skyhorsepublishing.com.

Visit our website at www.skyponypress.com.

10 9 8 7 6 5 4 3 2 1

Manufactured in China, October 2014
This product conforms to CPSIA 2008

Library of Congress Cataloging-in-Publication Data is available on file.

Cover design by Anthony Morais

ISBN: 978-1-62914-644-7
Ebook ISBN: 978-1-63220-203-1

The BIG BOOK of Presidents

From George Washington to Barack Obama

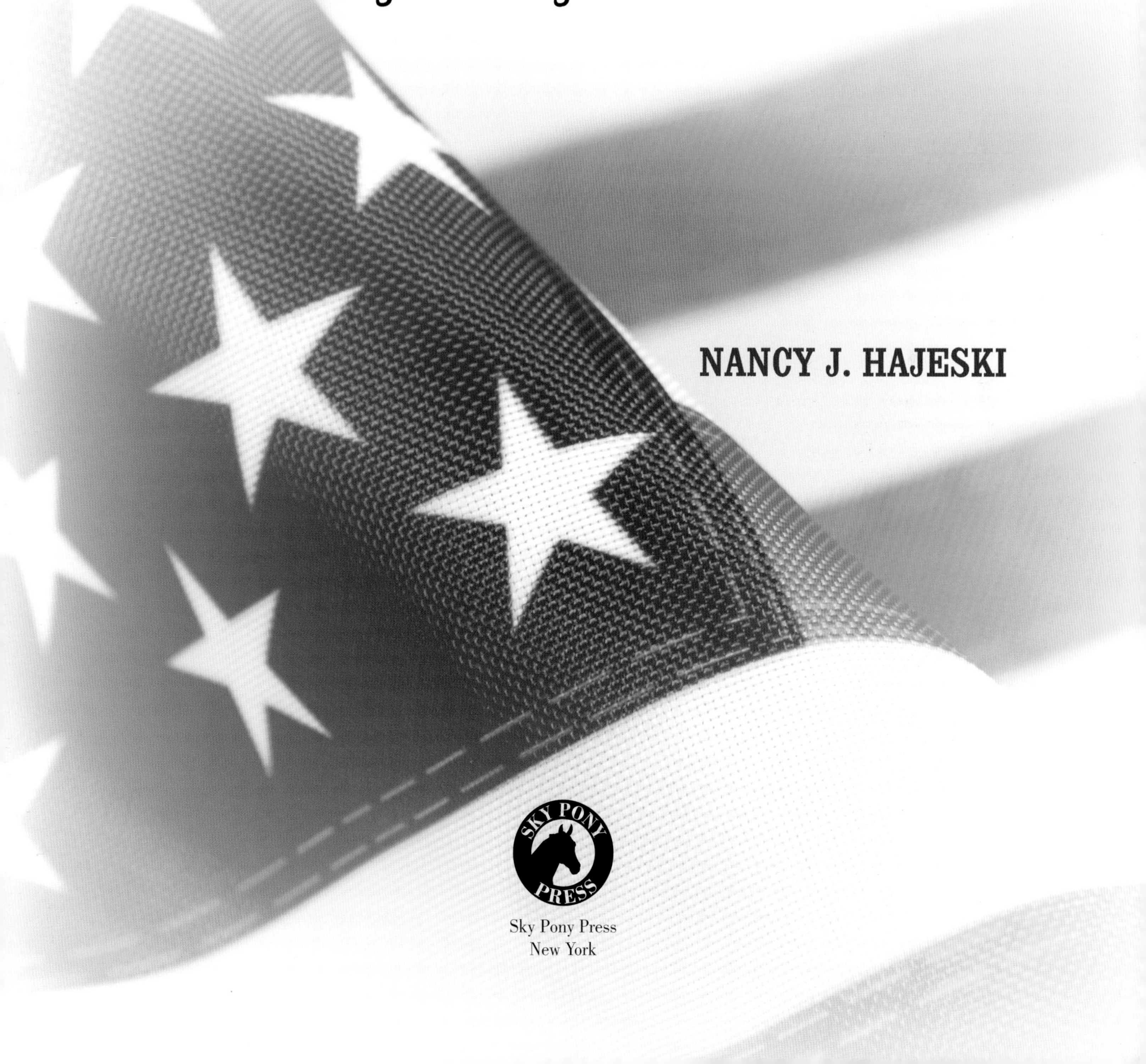

NANCY J. HAJESKI

Sky Pony Press
New York

Contents

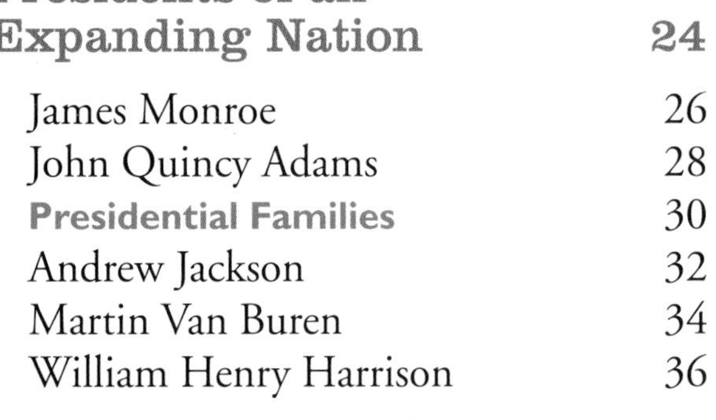

Ulysses S. Grant

Thomas Jefferson

Presidents of an Emerging Power 82

Cold War Presidents 104

Presidents in a Global Economy 124

Introduction: The American President

The president is the elected leader of the United States. The president represents the executive branch of the government, with the houses of Congress representing the legislative (lawmaking) branch and the Supreme Court representing the judicial branch. These three branches create a delicate balance of power. The chief executive is answerable to the other two branches, as they are answerable to the executive branch.

A Balance of Power

The nation's founders never intended to place a "leader for life" at the head of the country. After breaking free of the British monarchy, they knew that it would be foolish to adopt the same system that they had fought so hard to shed. But at the end of the Revolutionary War, the United States was in real need of leadership. The country entered a financial depression, and several states began to talk about leaving the Union. With little power and little money, the Continental Congress, the first government of the United States, was not a strong governing body. In 1787 the Constitutional Convention addressed this problem by forming a government that gave greater executive power to one individual but also included a system of checks and balances to prevent misuse of that power.

This new leader, unlike a king, queen, or other hereditary ruler, would serve for limited terms of four years. This "revolution by vote"—allowing citizens to change whole administrations at regular intervals—was a radical notion. Many nations considered it a noble experiment but one doomed to fail. They believed that strong presidents would declare themselves monarchs for life, and weak presidents would be thrown out of office. Yet this "experiment" in democracy has worked for more than two centuries and shows no sign of faltering.

The title of "president" came from the Continental Congress, whose head was called "President of the United States of America in Congress Assembled." This mouthful was usually shortened to "President of the United States." The Constitution also established that the president must be a natural-born citizen at least 35 years old and must have resided in the country for 14 years.

> **"A president's hardest task is not to do what is right but to know what is right."**
>
> **—Lyndon Baines Johnson**

Duties of the Office

The president's duties are varied, but they are also surprisingly limited. The president appoints ambassadors, judges of the federal courts, and members of the cabinet, a group of advisors. The president cannot introduce laws but can make a yearly agenda known to the Congress with the annual State of the Union Address. As commander in chief, the president oversees military actions and plans strategy, but the ability to declare war is in the hands of Congress. Although the president is also able to shape foreign policy and make treaties, any treaties must pass the Senate by a two-thirds vote.

Presidential Benefits

The presidential family, or first family, makes its home in the White House and is entitled to medical care, transportation, and kitchen and housekeeping services. Agents of the US Secret Service protect the president and first family, whether at home or abroad. The president also receives a salary. George W. Bush's 2007 salary was $400,000 per year, technically less than Washington's salary of $25,000, which translates in modern dollars to $566,000. Since 1959 all former presidents have received pensions, as well as travel expenses and mail privileges.

Two customized Boeing 747 airplanes fly the president wherever necessary. Whichever one carries the president is called "Air Force One" (as is any aircraft that carries the president). The personal presidential helicopter is known as "Marine One." Since 1954 the president's official musical anthem has been "Hail to the Chief," played to announce the president's appearance at public events.

Air Force One, the president's plane, flies over Mount Rushmore.

Gerald Ford consulting his advisors in the White House's Oval Office, where American presidents have conducted business since 1909.

Even presidents get to take vacations, and many return to their home states to relax. Others set up an informal "White House" at a favorite fishing, golfing, or hunting resort. The president's official country retreat is Camp David in Maryland. Originally called Shangri-la by Franklin Roosevelt, it was renamed by Dwight Eisenhower, in honor of his grandson David. Presidents have also used Camp David to host foreign dignitaries, starting with Winston Churchill in 1943.

Beginning with Herbert Hoover, retiring presidents have established presidential libraries in their home states. These libraries contain documents, artifacts, gifts of state, and museum exhibits, and they also offer public programs.

Today the president is recognized worldwide as the leader of a major economic and military power. Let us hope that future presidents will continue to use this power for the good of America and of all nations.

The Founding Presidents

George Washington, shown standing behind the desk at right, presides over the Constitutional Convention, which met in Philadelphia in 1787.

The founding presidents of the United States were George Washington, John Adams, Thomas Jefferson, and James Madison. All four had served in the Continental Congress and fought for freedom from British rule, either as soldiers or as legislators. Each one had great hopes for the new country, and each held a strong opinion on what direction the country should take.

At the end of the American Revolution, the United States no longer had a king to establish laws, collect taxes, oversee the military, create foreign policy, or keep the peace. For leadership the new nation immediately looked to its so-called Founding Fathers: patriots of wealth, education, courage, political experience, and—most importantly—high ideals.

> **"Human nature itself is evermore an advocate for liberty."**
>
> —John Adams

The Founders

As the victorious commander in chief of the Continental Army, George Washington was the natural choice to lead the nation, and the electoral college unanimously elected him president. Washington, like the Federalists, believed that a strong central government was best for the country. Yet he understood that the restrictions the Constitution placed on him—and all future presidents—also benefited the nation. He found the middle ground, creating a strong government that did not infringe on individual liberty. He was sure that the country should avoid party politics and that individual states should not put their own interests before that of the whole country.

John Adams was a Federalist . . . and also a realist. He believed that people are basically selfish and further acknowledged that social classes existed—"the gentlemen and the simple men"—and that an effective government must accept this reality. Adams preferred the idea of a republic run by learned men to Thomas Jefferson's broader ideal of a democracy ruled by the people. Jefferson broke with Washington on the issue of party politics and founded the Democratic-Republicans, who favored states' rights and opposed the Federalists. Jefferson argued that "the government that governed least, governed best." He also disagreed with Adams on human nature, believing that people were good and decent.

James Madison, another Republican for states' rights, carried on the reforms Jefferson began during his presidency. With his major roles in creating both the Constitution and the Bill of Rights, Madison was perhaps the most influential of the founding presidents in the long term.

Challenges to a New Nation

As war raged between England and France, the new country faced pressure to join in the fray. Washington and Jefferson managed to remain neutral, in spite of both countries' preying on American shipping. Adams, likewise, claimed his greatest accomplishment was avoiding war with France. Madison was no longer able to avoid war, though, and during his term the country took up arms against Britain in the War of 1812.

The founders all agreed on the issue of religious tolerance, one of the most important freedoms guaranteed by the Constitution. Washington was open-minded about religion and attended Quaker, German Reformed, and Roman Catholic services. Adams helped author the Massachusetts Constitution, which required local governments to pay for schooling in the Protestant religion. Adams explained to his critics that you don't have to believe in Protestantism, but if you want the good, fair-minded citizens that that religion inspires, you have to pay for it.

Even though he did not hold traditional religious beliefs, Jefferson was a staunch supporter of freedom of religion . . . or the freedom to have no religion at all. Madison added this caution: "And I have no doubt that every new example will succeed, as every past one has done, in showing that religion and Government will both exist in greater purity, the less they are mixed together."

These four remarkable men helped the country through its early growing pains and set the standards of behavior, diplomacy, and insight that many subsequent presidents have tried to emulate.

WHAT DOES THAT MEAN?

Democracy A system of government identified by majority rule, competitive elections, and freedom of speech and of the press

Electoral College A set of people who are empowered to elect a candidate to an office

Federalist A political party supporting the creation of a strong central government

Republic A state or country not led by a hereditary monarch and where the citizens have an impact on government

States' Rights A doctrine favoring the strict interpretation of the Constitution—limiting federal power and returning it to individual states

THE COLONIAL ALL-STARS

To better understand their roles, imagine the first four presidents in a sports competition. Washington is team captain (commander in chief and president), Adams is the star player who gets the ball rolling (pushes Congress for independence, heads the Declaration Committee), Jefferson writes the play book (the Declaration of Independence), and Madison acts as referee (determines how the rules should be interpreted by creating the Constitution and Bill of Rights).

1st President

George Washington

"The Father of His Country"

1789–1797

The measure of a great man is often that his character and his abilities match perfectly with the challenges that he is required to meet. George Washington was such a man. Tall and imposing, he seemed born to become "Father of His Country." As a military commander, he freed the 13 colonies from the grip of a tyrannical king. As the nation's first president, Washington guided it wisely through new and uncharted waters.

He was born in Westmoreland County to an aristocratic family of Virginia planters. In 1754 he received a commission as a lieutenant colonel and fought in the French and Indian War.

In 1759 Washington returned to his plantation near Mount Vernon and married a widow, Martha Dandridge Custis. Like many other planters, he was not happy with the harsh restrictions the British placed on the sale of American goods. He voiced these complaints in Virginia's House of Burgesses, though always in a moderate tone.

Commander in Chief

When the Second Continental Congress convened in Philadelphia in 1775, it elected Washington commander in chief of the Continental Army, and in July of that year he met his ragged troops for the first time in Cambridge, Massachusetts. In a campaign that ranged through most of the 13 colonies, Washington barely managed to avoid defeat. With the arrival of French allies, he was finally able to break the British hold. In 1781 he forced the surrender of General Cornwallis at Yorktown, Virginia.

"Associate with men of good quality if you esteem your own reputation; for it is better to be alone than in bad company."

Although America's independence was soon established, the nation was not prospering, so in 1787 Washington attended the Constitutional Convention in Philadelphia to help draft rules for a new government. After the Constitution was approved, the electoral college unanimously elected Washington first president of the United States.

During his two terms Washington recognized and respected that the Constitution gave national policy-making power to the Congress. Foreign policy, on the other hand, became a major concern to him. Near the end of his first term, to Washington's dismay, two political parties began to form. Afraid that this might lead to national discord, he warned against "excessive party spirit and geographical distinctions" in his Farewell Address.

After his presidency, Washington returned to Mount Vernon. Three years later he suffered a serious throat infection and died. The national mourning went on for months. The country's new capital was called Washington in his honor.

BIOGRAPHICAL FACTS

Birth February 22, 1732, Pope's Creek, Westmoreland County, Virginia
Religion Anglican/Episcopalian
Education Private tutors
Occupation Surveyor; soldier; planter
Other Offices Member of Virginia House of Burgesses; member of Continental Congress; chairman of Constitutional Convention
Military Service Lieutenant colonel in French and Indian War; aide to General Braddock; commander in chief of Continental Army
Political Party No party affiliation
Vice President John Adams
Age at Inauguration 57
Death December 14, 1799, Mount Vernon, Virginia

Martha Washington was known in her lifetime as "Lady Washington."

"My mother was the most beautiful woman I ever saw. All I am I owe to my mother. I attribute all my success in life to the moral, intellectual and physical education I received from her."

—George Washington

Mount Rushmore's image of George Washington.

DID YOU KNOW . . . ?

- Washington was the first president to free his slaves.
- His inaugural speech became a tradition and set the bar for other presidents who followed him.
- Nelson, a handsome bay, was the president's favorite mount and became America's "First Horse."
- Washington's favorite foods were ice cream and fish.
- Washington's image has appeared on the dollar bill, the quarter, and many postage stamps.
- Washington is one of the four presidents whose face is carved into Mount Rushmore.

THE WASHINGTON FAMILY

Father Augustine Washington (1694–1743)
Occupation Planter
Mother Mary Ball Washington (1708–1789)
Wife Martha Dandridge Custis
Birth June 21, 1731, Kent County, Virginia
Marriage January 6, 1759
Death May 22, 1802, Mount Vernon, Virginia
Stepchildren John "Jack" Parke Custis (1754–1781); Martha "Patsy" Custis (1756–1773)
Grandchildren Eleanor "Nelly" Parke Custis (1779–1852); George Washington "Little Wash" Parke Custis (1781–1857)

The Washingtons with "Little Wash," Nelly, and servant William Lee.

In 1848 construction began on a soaring monument to honor the nation's most cherished founding president. At its completion the Washington Monument was the tallest structure in the country.

WASHINGTON THE GENERAL

October 17, 1781, Lord Cornwallis of Britain surrenders his army to General Washington at Yorktown, Virginia. With the aid of French allies, Washington had secured a revolutionary victory for the colonies.

In 1776, with the arrival of 30,000 British troops in New York and the adoption of the Declaration of Independence, the Revolutionary War was intensifying. General Washington knew he would be leading his untried troops into battle against seasoned British soldiers and fierce Hessian mercenaries. Realizing that his army was not trained for traditional combat, Washington made a fateful decision. He would have his troops attack the British and then fall back. In a report to Congress, he wrote, "we should on all Occasions avoid a general Action, or put anything to the Risque, unless compelled by a necessity, into which we ought never to be drawn." The more regimented British generals were not accustomed to this strike-and-retreat type of warfare; it wasn't "sporting." In spite of Washington's tactics, his men battled for six long years against far greater numbers, enduring much hardship and deprivation.

WASHINGTON AVOIDS ANOTHER WAR

After the French Revolution led to war between England and France, Washington found himself caught between his secretary of state, Thomas Jefferson, who favored the French, and his secretary of the treasury, Alexander Hamilton, who was for the British. Washington chose to remain neutral, allowing the county to find its footing before engaging in any further conflicts.

Thomas Jefferson, shown standing, served as the United States' first secretary of state. Alexander Hamilton, seated third from left, served as the first secretary of the treasury.

"Humanity has won its battle. Liberty now has a country."

—Marquis de Lafayette

WASHINGTON THE SURVEYOR

George Washington's boyhood home lay at the edge of a wilderness that stretched 2,500 miles, all the way to the Pacific Ocean. As a young man of 16, Washington crossed the frontier on several surveying expeditions for Thomas, Lord Fairfax. It's possible that these glimpses of a rugged and endless paradise showed him the true potential of America—both for exploration and expansion.

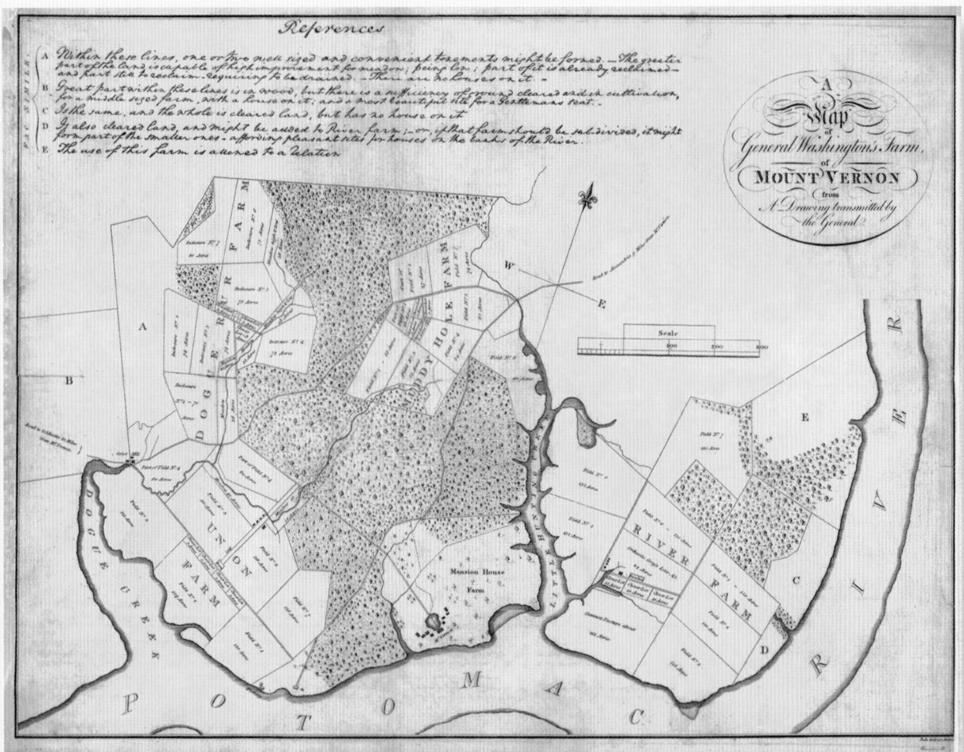

Washington drew on his early surveying experience to make this map of his Mount Vernon plantation.

MARQUIS DE LAFAYETTE

When the Marquis de Lafayette, a young French nobleman, learned of the 13 colonies' struggle for independence, he resolved to help them. In 1777 he landed in Philadelphia, where the Continental Congress, impressed by his fervor for the American cause, commissioned him a major general. Lafayette served on George Washington's staff, and the two men became lifelong friends. Lafayette refused to support a group of officers who were trying to have Washington relieved of duty. Lafayette returned to France, intent on gaining French support and funding for the Revolution. In 1780 French ships arrived in America with troops and supplies.

French aristocrat Gilbert du Motier, Marquis de Lafayette, so believed in the revolutionary cause that he agreed to serve in both the American and French revolutions.

Timeline of the Washington Presidency

US Events / **World Events**

1789 (US) Delaware outlaws the African slave trade

1789 (World) French Revolution begins with the storming of the Bastille, a notorious prison in Paris, on July 14

1789 (World) The *celerifere* or *velocifere*, an early version of the bicycle without pedals, is invented in France

1790 (US) Washington signs the first US patent, issued to Samuel Hopkins for his method of making potash and pearlash, two compounds used in agriculture

1791 (World) Tom Paine publishes *Rights of Man*

1792 (US) Kentucky admitted to the Union

1792 (US) Congress establishes the post office

1793 (World) King Louis XVI of France beheaded by guillotine

1793 (US) Eli Whitney invents the cotton gin, which processes raw cotton

1796 (US) E Pluribus Unum ("Out of Many, One") is added to US coins

1796 (World) English physician Edward Jenner gives an eight-year-old boy the first smallpox vaccination

2nd President

John Adams

"The Colossus of Independence"

1797–1801

John Adams was argumentative, headstrong, and a little sensitive, especially about his short stature. Yet Adams brought such fierce determination to the cause of American liberty that he stands shoulder to shoulder with George Washington, Thomas Jefferson, and Benjamin Franklin as a founder of the United States.

Early Years

Born in Braintree, Massachusetts, Adams was the son of a farmer. He attended Harvard College and chose to teach for several years before studying law. It was his habit to write down his impressions of events and people, a custom that served him well as a lawyer. One case he reported on was James Otis's argument on the legality of the writs of assistance—warrants that allowed officers of the British Crown to search any property or person. Adams, along with many other colonists, objected to this gross misuse of power, which inflamed his growing resentment against British rule.

In Abigail Smith, the daughter of a minister from Weymouth, Massachusetts, Adams found his soul mate. Through long separations, the couple kept up a steady and intimate correspondence.

As delegate to the First and Second Continental Congress, Adams was the leading voice for the cause of independence. During the war the government sent him on diplomatic missions to France and Holland, where he borrowed funds to finance the Revolution. He also helped negotiate the Treaty of Paris in 1783, which ended the war.

An Uneasy Partnership

Adams served two terms as vice president under Washington, chafing at the position, which left him with little to do. In 1796 he was elected president, with Thomas Jefferson, from the opposing party, as his vice president. It was not a happy partnership.

Like Washington, Adams took a strong role in American foreign policy, negotiating with both the British and French to stop the seizing of American merchant ships. His term was marked by the building up of the military and the passing of the Alien and Sedition Acts—aimed at foreign immigrants and domestic adversaries. Adams narrowly lost the election of 1800 to Jefferson, which increased the rift between the two men.

"People and nations are forged in the fires of adversity."

Twelve years later Adams and Jefferson made up, and when Adams died on July 4, 1826—on the 50th anniversary of the signing of the Declaration of Independence—his last words were, "Thomas Jefferson survives." He could not know that Jefferson had died at Monticello only hours earlier.

Adams lived long enough to see his son John Quincy become the sixth United States president.

BIOGRAPHICAL FACTS

Birth October 30, 1735, Braintree (now Quincy), Massachusetts

Religion Congregationalist/Unitarian

Education Harvard College (graduated 1755)

Occupation Teacher; lawyer

Other Offices Member of Continental Congress; commissioner to France; minister to the Netherlands; minister to England; vice president

Political Party Federalist

Vice President Thomas Jefferson

Age at Inauguration 61

Death July 4, 1826, Braintree, Massachusetts

Abigail Adams, witty and independent, championed the rights of women, writing to her husband at the Constitutional Convention to "Remember the Ladies."

"Do not put such unlimited power into the hands of the husbands. Remember all men would be tyrants if they could."

—Abigail Adams, to John, who was drafting the Constitution

DID YOU KNOW . . . ?

- John and Abigail Adams were the first presidential couple to move into the White House. Since the building was under construction and the yard was muddy, Abigail hung her wet laundry in the Blue Room to dry.
- After he suggested addressing new president Washington as "His Majesty," the stout Adams quickly gained the nickname "His Rotundity."
- Adams's favorite horse was named Cleopatra.
- Adams's crypt is at United First Parish Church in Quincy, known as the Church of the Presidents.
- Adams, who died at age 90, was the longest-lived person to be elected to both the vice presidency and the presidency.

THE ADAMS FAMILY

Father John Adams (1691–1761)

Occupation Farmer

Mother Susanna Boylston Adams (1709–1797)

Wife Abigail Smith Adams

Birth November 23, 1744, Weymouth, Massachusetts

Marriage October 25, 1764

Death October 28, 1818, Braintree, Massachusetts

Children Abigail Amelia (1765–1813); John Quincy (1767–1848); Susannah (1768–1770); Charles (1770–1800); Thomas Boylston (1772–1832); Elizabeth (1775)

John Quincy, Adams's oldest son.

Timeline of the Adams Presidency

US Events | **World Events**

1797 (World) Jumping from a hot-air balloon 3,200 feet above Paris, André-Jacques Garnerin makes the first recorded parachute dive.

1798 (US) Congress passes Alien and Sedition Acts aimed at foreign and domestic adversaries

1799 (World) Napoleon made First Consul of France

1799 (World) German-born Sir Frederick William Herschel of England discovers infrared light

1799 (World) Discovery of the Rosetta Stone

1800 (US) Library of Congress founded

1800 (World) Metric system made law in France

1800 (US) Capital of United States moves from Philadelphia to Washington, DC

1800 (World) The clothes dryer invented in France and England

1800 (World) Italian Alessandro Volta invents electric battery

1800 (US) Robert Fulton, developer of the steamboat, builds the *Nautilus*, an early submarine

1800 (World) World population is 870 million

The White House Story

George Washington and White House competition-winning architect James Hoban overseeing the building's construction.

The White House is more than just the home of the president and his family. It is the president's business office, his "embassy" when meeting foreign dignitaries, and often his refuge.

Design Competition

Although he never lived in it, George Washington came up with the idea of a formal presidential residence. In 1790 he signed an act of Congress to create a federal district "not more than ten miles square on the River Potomac." As Washington walked the area with city planner Pierre-Charles L'Enfant, his gaze was drawn to a small, scenic hill beside Goose Creek. This, he decided, would be the site of the residence.

Nine architects (including an anonymous Thomas Jefferson) submitted proposals to a competition held to determine the plan for the building. Washington chose James Hoban's design for a simple, elegant, three-story structure finished in pale sandstone. At Washington's urging, Irish-born Hoban increased the size and added a large reception area, the East Room.

Construction began in 1792. Scottish immigrants laid the walls, and Italian and Irish workers bricked and plastered them. When money ran short, the design changed to two stories, as it remains today, although there are actually six levels. In the late 1820s the North and South Porticos were added.

"I pray Heaven to bestow the Blessings on this House and all that shall hereafter inhabit it. May none but honest and wise Men ever rule under this roof."

—John Adams, in a letter to Abigail

Moving In

John Adams was the first president to reside in the house, then called the Presidential Palace. He was not impressed with the unplastered walls or the noise of workmen.

Jefferson held an open house in the mansion to celebrate his inauguration, and this practice became a tradition. By Lincoln's time the celebration had gotten out of hand, with guests spilling out onto the lawns. During Grover Cleveland's first inauguration, he reviewed the troops from a flag-draped platform in front of the White House. This gave rise to the inaugural parade that ends with the new president taking the oath of office.

Home Improvement

In 1891 President Theodore Roosevelt carried out a White House renovation and expansion, which included the construction of the West Wing, home to the Oval Office where the president conducts the business of state.

Eventually, the many additions to the wood-frame building took a toll, and in 1948, during the term of Harry Truman, the White House was in danger of collapse. The Trumans moved to nearby Blair House, as workers installed an internal steel frame and reconstructed all the rooms. They also dug two sub-basements, along with a bomb shelter—a sign of the Cold War times.

Saving History

Its cramped and shabby living quarters, infested with rats, inspired First Lady Caroline Harrison to draw up plans for a renovation of the White House. She never got approval for her plan but did undertake an important project, cataloging furniture, pictures, and decorative objects of historic value in the mansion, ensuring their preservation.

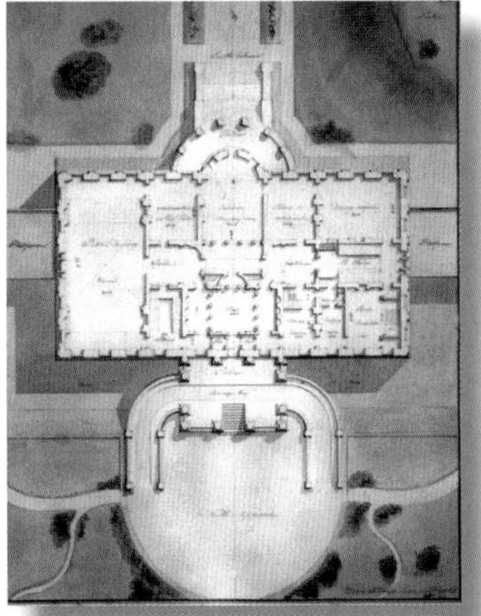

Caroline Harrison's renovation plan.

WHITE HOUSE FACTS

The complex consists of the Executive Residence and the East and West Wings. Frederick Law Olmsted designed the landscaped grounds, which now contain a number of gardens, including the famous Rose Garden—created by First Lady Louise Wilson in 1913—and the Jacqueline Kennedy Garden. Among the oldest trees on the property are magnolias planted by Andrew Jackson. The sweeping South Lawn is used for public events.

DID YOU KNOW . . . ?

- The White House has 132 rooms, 35 bathrooms, and 6 levels in the residence. There are also 412 doors, 147 windows, 28 fireplaces, 8 staircases, and 3 elevators.
- It's been called the "President's Palace," the "President's House," and the "Executive Mansion." Theodore Roosevelt officially dubbed it the "White House" in 1901.
- With five full-time chefs, the White House kitchen is able to serve dinner to as many as 140 guests and hors d'oeuvres to more than 1,000 . . . and can rustle up a grilled cheese sandwich in the middle of the night.
- The White House requires 570 gallons of paint to cover its outside surface.
- The White House has a variety of recreation facilities, including a tennis court, jogging track, swimming pool, movie theater, and bowling alley.

Interior Design

The White House interior has gone through many alterations, based on the tastes of the time, from elegant Federal furnishings to fussy Victorian clutter. In the 1960s stylish Jacqueline Kennedy restored many of the historic objects that had been packed away or sold, designating a period theme for each room. When the work was completed, the first lady gave a TV tour of the redecorated White House. Sales of the guidebook helped fund the restoration.

The Blue Room in 1962, featuring portraits of past presidents.

The Red Room after refurbishing in 1962.

A jubilant crowd descends on the White House for Andrew Jackson's 1829 inaugural reception.

Good Times and Bad

The White House has been the scene of many joyful occasions, from engagements and marriages to births and birthday parties, as well as somber ones. Eight presidents and three first ladies died while living there, as did a number of presidential children. Abraham Lincoln laid in state (on view for public tribute) in the East Room after his assassination, and so did William McKinley. John F. Kennedy's body was brought there from Dallas before public viewing in the Rotunda of the Capitol.

Thomas Jefferson

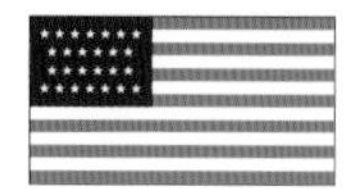

"The Man of the People"

1801–1809

Thomas Jefferson was a true Renaissance man—architect, musician, horticulturist, author, and inventor. By birth Jefferson was an American aristocrat, yet he spent his life working toward the causes of liberty and religious tolerance.

Jefferson was born in Albemarle County, Virginia, to a prominent family of planters. An avid student, Jefferson received a classical education from private tutors, and after graduating from the College of William and Mary, he read law. His Palladian-style home, Monticello, was still under construction when he courted and married Martha Skelton, a young widow. She died after giving birth to their sixth child, and Jefferson never remarried.

As a member of Virginia's House of Burgesses, Jefferson was asked to attend the Continental Congress in Philadelphia. Jefferson was not known as a great speaker, but he more than made up for this with his ability as a writer. It was "Long Tom" the Congress turned to when it was time to specify the reasons for declaring independence from Great Britain. Jefferson became Virginia's governor during the American Revolution, and in 1785 he replaced Benjamin Franklin as minister to France. His love of the French people led Jefferson to sympathize with France's own revolution.

Leading the Democratic-Republicans

During Washington's presidency two conflicting political parties formed: the Federalists, who favored a strong central government, and the Democratic-Republicans, who believed in the rights of the states. Jefferson soon became the leader of the Democratic-Republicans, and in 1796 they offered him the nomination for president. He lost to John Adams by three votes. Although a member of the opposing party, Jefferson was declared vice president. In 1800 voters elected him president.

As president Jefferson cut military spending, drastically trimmed the budget, eliminated an unpopular whiskey tax, and still managed to reduce the national debt by a third. During his second term, as the Napoleonic War raged in Europe, he tried to remain neutral, caught between England and France as both countries continued to harass US merchant ships. His solution, ultimately an unpopular one, was to declare an embargo, or legal prohibition on commerce, on American shipping.

"Every generation needs a new revolution."

After two terms Jefferson retired to Monticello, where he continued to follow public affairs. He was the founder and architect of the University of Virginia, which was the first university in the United States to separate education from the teaching of religion. The campus he created was designed around a library rather than a church.

Thomas Jefferson died on July 4, 1826, the very same day that friend and rival John Adams died.

Thomas Jefferson designed his estate, Monticello, in a classical style. The impressive domed house sits on the summit of an 850-foot-high peak in the mountains near Charlottesville, Virginia. *Monticello* is Italian for "little mountain."

THE LOUISIANA PURCHASE

In 1803 Napoleon Bonaparte, who needed money to fund his attempted conquest of Europe, offered Jefferson a large area of French-held North America. The president managed to put his country's future above his private belief that such an act might not be constitutional. With the completion of the Louisiana Purchase in 1804, the United States nearly doubled in size. Jefferson sent two intrepid men, Captain Meriwether Lewis and William Clark, to explore and map the new territory with their "Corps of Discovery." They hired a Native American woman, Sacagawea of the Shoshone tribe, to serve as their interpreter and guide.

A statue of Sacagawea, the Shoshone woman who guided the Corps of Discovery of Lewis and Clark.

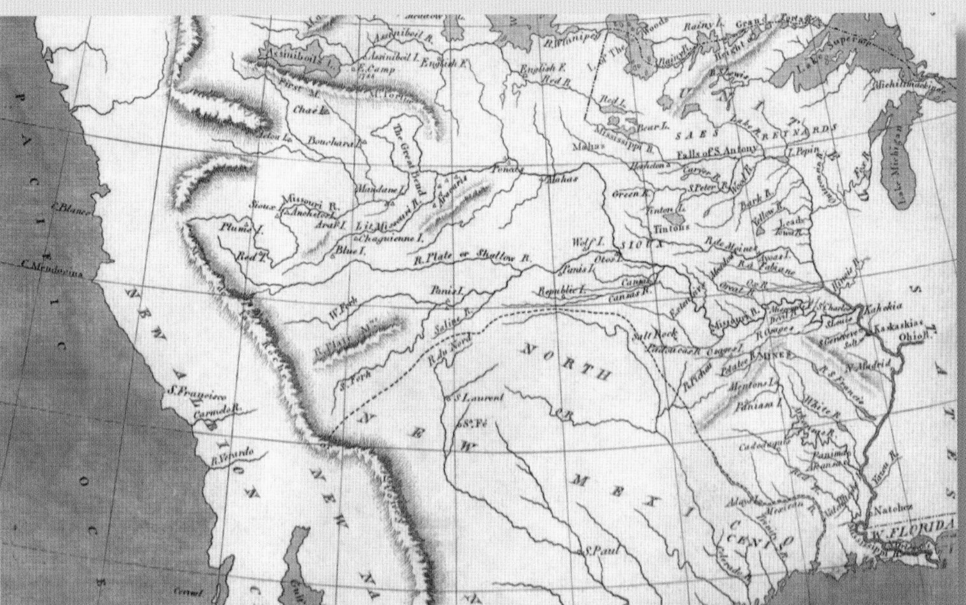

A map drawn soon after Jefferson authorized the Louisiana Purchase, which nearly doubled the nation's size.

Timeline of the Jefferson Presidency

US Events | **World Events**

1801–1805 (World)
First Barbary War; US warships sent to the Mediterranean

1802 (World)
Madame Tussaud's wax museum opens in London

1803 (US)
Chief Kamehameha unites the Sandwich (Hawaiian) Islands

1804 (US)
Alexander Hamilton and Aaron Burr duel; Hamilton dies from wounds

1804 (US)
Louisiana Purchase from France

1804 (World)
In England, Richard Trevithick's steam locomotive makes the first locomotive journey

1804–1806 (US)
Lewis and Clark expedition explores land acquired in the Louisiana Purchase

1804 (World)
Napoleon Bonaparte becomes emperor of France

1805 (US)
American inventor Oliver Evans designs the first icebox

1807 (US)
Benjamin Silliman, a professor of chemistry at Yale, invents soda water

1807 (US)
Robert Fulton debuts steamboat *Clermont*

1807 (World)
British Empire abolishes its slave trade

1808 (US)
Congress prohibits importing African slaves

James Madison

"The Father of the Constitution" **1809–1817**

James Madison was small in stature and in portraits appears old before his time. Writer Washington Irving called him "a withered little apple-John." Yet he brought great energy to his undertakings, making major contributions to both the Constitution and the Bill of Rights. As president he guided the country through a controversial war.

"The advice nearest to my heart . . . is that the Union of the States be cherished and perpetuated."

Early Political Life

Madison grew up in Orange County, Virginia, where his parents owned a prosperous tobacco plantation and many slaves. He studied at the College of New Jersey and was a member of the Virginia Legislature. He also served in the Continental Congress, where he was a renowned debater. In 1787, while at the Constitutional Convention in New York, he drafted the Virginia Plan—including the outline for a three-branch system of government—which became the basis of the US Constitution. In later years when anyone called him the "Father of the Constitution," he was quick to point out that it was the work of "many heads and many hands."

In 1789 Madison was elected to the House of Representatives. He was not at first convinced of the need for a Bill of Rights but later reversed his stand and submitted 12 amendments protecting the civil rights of citizens. Ten of these were accepted as the Bill of Rights in 1791.

In 1794 Madison married Dolley Payne Todd, a lively, charming, and much younger woman. During his presidency, she entertained Washington society and advised her husband on running the country.

A War President

Madison served as Jefferson's secretary of state and helped negotiate the Louisiana Purchase. When he was elected president in 1808, his chief concern was British harassment of US merchant shipping. Madison began to drum up support for a war. Unfortunately he did not spend as much effort building up the military, and when Congress declared war in 1812, the country found itself unprepared. American forces suffered a number of defeats, and British troops marched on Washington and burned the White House. In spite of the United States' poor showing in the war, at its end a wave of nationalism, or intense loyalty to the nation, swept the country and Madison's popularity soared.

After his second term he returned to his home, Montpelier; both his plantation and his health were failing. At age 78 he worked on the revision of the Virginia Constitution. Madison died at Montpelier in 1836, the last remaining signer of the Constitution he had fought to conceive.

BIOGRAPHICAL FACTS

Birth March 16, 1751, Port Conway, Virginia

Religion Anglican/Episcopalian

Education College of New Jersey (now Princeton University; graduated 1761)

Occupation Planter

Other Offices Member of Continental Congress; member of Virginia legislature; member of Constitutional Convention; member of US House of Representatives; secretary of state

Political Party Democratic-Republican

Vice President George Clinton; Elbridge Gerry

Age at Inauguration 57

Death June 23, 1836, Orange County, Virginia

The artist Charles Wilson Peale painted this miniature portrait of James Madison in 1783. Madison mounted it on a pin and gave it to his then fiancée, Kitty Floyd. Kitty later returned it to James when she broke their engagement.

THE MADISON FAMILY

Father James Madison (1723–1801)

Occupation Tobacco planter

Mother Eleanor Conway Madison (1731–1829)

Wife Dolley Payne Todd Madison

Birth May 29, 1768, New Garden, North Carolina

Marriage September 15, 1894

Death July 12, 1849, Washington, DC

Stepson John Payne Todd (1792–1852)

MRS. MADISON: THE "MAGNIFICENT DOLL"

Dolley Madison served as White House hostess to both Thomas
Jefferson and her husband. An upbeat and charming woman, Dolley skillfully entertained many important visitors. She can truly be called the first "first lady," in the sense that the role is viewed today.

During the War of 1812, with
British troops threatening to burn down the president's home, Dolley sealed her fame by courageously
saving a number of treasures from the White House, including the famous Gilbert Stuart portrait of George Washington.

Known for her sparkling personality (and love of feathered turbans), Dolley Madison ruled as leader of the Washington, DC, social circle for 50 years.

Timeline of the Madison Presidency

US Events | **World Events**

1809 (World) Englishman Humphry Davy invents arc lamp

1810 (World) Yellow fever epidemic kills 25,000 in Spain

1811 (US) American forces led by William Henry Harrison defeat Indians in Battle of Tippecanoe

1811 (World) British author Jane Austen publishes *Sense and Sensibility*

1811–1817 (World) Venezuela, Paraguay, Uruguay, Chile, Brazil, Argentina declare independence from Spain

1812 (US) Louisiana admitted to Union

1812 (US) The United States declares war against Great Britain

1812 (US) Cannonballs bounce off the sides of the USS *Constitution* during its battle with the British *Guerriere*, earning it its nickname "Old Ironsides"

1813 (World) Johann Wyss publishes *The Swiss Family Robinson*

1814 (World) Treaty of Ghent ends War of 1812

1814 (World) First sales of canned food

1816 (US) Bank of the United States signed into law

Presidents of an Expanding Nation

In a painting by John Gast called *American Progress*, Native Americans and wild animals flee as settlers travel westward, bringing with them the trappings of civilization, such as schools, telegraph wires, and steam locomotives. Columbia, the personification of the United States, leads the settlers.

It may seem odd now, with the United States stretching "from sea to shining sea," that the nation began as a cluster of states on the Eastern Seaboard. But when George Washington took office, much of North America was undeveloped, inhabited by wild animals and sometimes-hostile Native Americans. Trappers and surveyors ventured into this wilderness, but it was not welcoming to homesteaders. And even though the United States did gain British-held territories at the end of the Revolution, Spain had holdings in Florida and the Southwest, and France soon regained control of the vast Louisiana Territory west of the Mississippi. These foreign-held territories remained impediments, and it was up to future presidents to acquire them so that the country could expand.

"Go West, young man, and grow up with the country."

—John B. L. Soule, editor of the *Terre Haute Express*

Jefferson had taken the first step—by completing the acquisition of the Louisiana Purchase from France, he nearly doubled the nation's size. Other large portions of land would later be added to the country with the purchase of the Oregon Country and the Mexican Cession in the 1840s.

In order to safeguard American expansion, in

1823 James Monroe warned other nations, in a statement that became known as the Monroe Doctrine, that any interference with or influence on the independent nations of North and South America would be considered an act of hostility.

The government understood that acquiring territory was pointless unless it could be put to use, so it encouraged the settlement of new lands. John Quincy Adams opened up the Cumberland Road to Ohio, while experienced woodsmen, most notably Daniel Boone, had already begun opening up areas of Tennessee and Kentucky. Thousands of settlers followed in their wake. Stagecoach companies, funded by mail contracts, turned narrow hunting trails into usable roads. The military built forts along the frontier that offered a sense of safety to nearby settlements.

Eventually many territories outside the borders of the United States applied for statehood. For some the process began with the creation of territorial governments followed by delegations to Congress. Others applicants, such as Texas, were independent nations before becoming states.

Opening Up the West

In 1838 the first real migrations west began. Long trains of pioneer families in Conestoga wagons set off from eastern hubs, such as St. Louis, Missouri, seeking a new life on the prairies. John Tyler's "Log Cabin" bill in the 1840s entitled settlers to claim 160 acres of land with deferred payment before it was offered for public sale.

Native Americans continued to try to stem the tide of settlers moving westward. A number of tribes fought back when they saw their hunting grounds and sacred burial grounds taken over by land developers. The US government made peace treaties with the various tribes, yet many of the treaties were broken—often by the Americans. The natural resources on Native American land—including beaver, mink, hardwood lumber, gold, and silver—were too tempting for many settlers to ignore. Far too often a treaty made in Washington, DC, did nothing to discourage a beaver trapper in Missouri or a gold miner in South Dakota.

During Andrew Jackson's presidency, Indian removal was carried out with harsh, even deadly efficiency. The government relocated tribes to distant, often infertile, locations. The woodland Cherokee, for example, were forced to move to the plains of Oklahoma. It is not surprising that Indians frequently left the reservations, in spite of reprisals from the federal army.

By the middle of the 19th century, many Americans had begun to believe that this westward expansion toward the Pacific Ocean was an obvious course and their right under nature. This notion of a "Manifest Destiny" later became an excuse for expansion outside of the United States.

WHAT DOES THAT MEAN?

American System A tariff, or tax placed on foreign goods, intended to encourage American manufacturers

Conestoga Wagon A heavy, broad-wheeled covered wagon drawn by four to eight mules or four to six oxen that could transport loads up to seven tons

Gag Rule The prohibition against discussing anti-slavery petitions in Congress from 1835 to 1844

Manifest Destiny The belief that the United States was destined to extend from ocean to ocean

Monroe Doctrine A doctrine issued in 1823 proclaiming that the United States would no longer tolerate European powers colonizing or interfering with the affairs of the Americas

Nullification Crisis The controversy started by South Carolina's refusal to recognize or enforce a federal tariff within its boundaries

Second Party System The US political system from about 1837 to 1852, characterized by high voter turnouts and intense party loyalty

SHIFTING FRONTIERS

In the United States, the term "frontier"—from the French word for borderland—came to mean the zone running between the settled lands and the wilderness. In the central Atlantic states, the frontier was to the west, in the Pacific regions it was to the east, and in New England it was to the north. With each successive president the frontier was pushed farther back.

James Monroe

"The Last Cocked Hat" **1817–1825**

Monroe was a quiet, capable man, who through most of his life maintained a spotless reputation. History best remembers him for his attempts to prevent the spread of slavery and for his belief that the undeveloped parts of the United States must remain free of foreign influence.

Born in Westmoreland County, Virginia, the son of a tobacco planter and slaveholder, Monroe attended the College of William and Mary and served with distinction in the Continental Army. He was wounded in the shoulder during the Battle of Trenton in New Jersey.

As a fellow Virginian, he was sympathetic with Jefferson's anti-Federalist policies, and in 1790 he was elected US senator. He went on to hold a number of political and diplomatic offices, including minister to France under Washington, governor of Virginia, minister to Great Britain under Jefferson, and secretary of state for Madison. Madison also appointed him secretary of war from 1814 to 1815.

After holding two simultaneous cabinet posts, Monroe created a strong cabinet for his own term of office. With an eye to the geography of politics, Monroe appointed Southerner John C. Calhoun as secretary of war and Northerner John Quincy Adams as secretary of state. This move eased political tensions and created the "Era of Good Feelings."

A bitter quarrel began in Congress when the Missouri Territory applied for entry into the Union as a slave state in 1819. Two years later the Missouri Compromise recognized Missouri as a slave state but accepted Maine as a free state and further banned slavery to the north and west of Missouri.

The Monroe Doctrine

In an 1823 speech to Congress, the president outlined his concept—the Monroe Doctrine—that the Americas must remain free of European colonization or influence and that any attempts to the contrary would be considered acts of hostility.

"Our country may be likened to a new house. We lack many things, but we possess the most precious of all—liberty!"

After the end of his second term, Monroe and his family lived at both Oak Hill and at Monroe Hill at the University of Virginia. When Monroe's wife, Elizabeth, died in 1830, Monroe moved in with his daughter Maria and her husband, Samuel L. Gouverneur (who had been married in the first White House wedding), in New York City. He died of tuberculosis on July 4, 1831, the third president to succumb on that historic anniversary.

BIOGRAPHICAL FACTS

Birth April 28th, 1758, Westmoreland County, Virginia
Religion Anglican/Episcopalian
Education College of William and Mary
Occupation Planter
Other Offices Member of Continental Congress; US senator; minister to France; minister to England; governor of Virginia; secretary of state; secretary of war
Military Service Lieutenant colonel, Continental Army
Political Party Democratic-Republican
Vice President Daniel D. Tompkins
Age at Inauguration 58
Death July 4, 1831, New York, New York

Monroe appears holding the flag behind Washington in the famous painting *Washington Crossing the Delaware.*

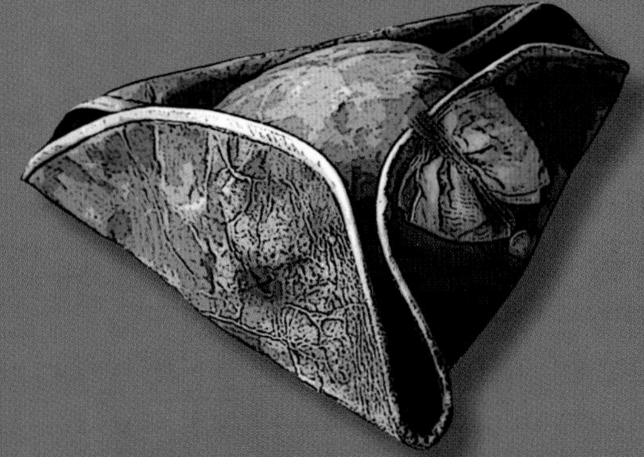

A military cocked hat from the 18th century. A symbol of Revolutionary War patriots, it was a round hat with the sides folded up and tied with a bow. Monroe was the last president to wear the style, which is why historians call him the "Last Cocked Hat."

"Monroe was so honest that if you turned his soul inside out there would not be a spot on it."

—Thomas Jefferson

DID YOU KNOW...?

- The African nation Liberia, founded as a haven for freed slaves, named its capital Monrovia in Monroe's honor.
- Monroe was the last president to fight in the Revolutionary War.
- Monroe's likeness appeared in more than 350 paintings throughout the 1800s.

THE MONROE FAMILY

Father Spence Monroe (d. 1774)
Occupation Tobacco planter
Mother Elizabeth Jones Monroe (d. before 1774)
Wife Elizabeth "Eliza" Kortright
Birth June 30, 1768, New York, New York
Marriage February 16, 1786
Death September 23, 1830, Oak Hill, Virginia
Children Eliza (1786–1835); James (1799–1800); Maria (1803–1850)

While Monroe was ambassador to France, Elizabeth Monroe helped free the wife of the Marquis de Lafayette from prison during the Reign of Terror. The French called Elizabeth "la belle Americaine," which means "the beautiful American."

Timeline of the Monroe Presidency

US Events | **World Events**

1816 (US) Indiana admitted to the Union

1817 (US) Construction begins on the Erie Canal

1818 (World) British doctor James Blundell performs the first successful blood transfusion

1818 (US) Illinois admitted to the Union

1818 (World) British author Mary Shelley publishes *Frankenstein, or, The Modern Prometheus*

1819 (US) US acquires Florida from Spain

1820 (World) George III, the last British monarch to rule the American colonies, dies

1820 (US) Maine admitted as a free state; Missouri Compromise is passed to admit Missouri as a slave state

1821 (World) Mexico declares independence from Spain

1824 (World) The Royal Society for the Prevention of Cruelty to Animals (RSPCA) founded in England

1824 (US) William Austin Burt receives a patent for his typographer, a forerunner of the typewriter

1824 (World) First commercial pasta factory in Italy

John Quincy Adams

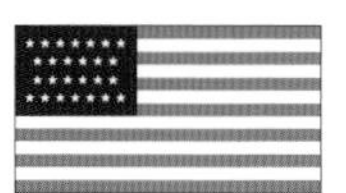

"Old Man Eloquent" **1825–1829**

John Quincy Adams shared many traits with his patriot father, including a hasty temper and high ideals—and his relatively short stature. Their political careers even ran parallel: lawyer, ambassador, and president. Like his father, he also served one unpopular term, but he then went on to become a leading voice in Congress against slavery.

Born at the Adams family farm in Braintree, John Quincy studied law at Harvard. When he was 26 George Washington appointed him minister to the Netherlands. He served in the Senate for six years and then as minister to Russia. On Adams's return, James Monroe appointed him secretary of state. In this role young Adams hit his stride, negotiating with England for the joint occupation of the Oregon Territory, overseeing the acquisition of Florida from Spain, and helping to create the Monroe Doctrine.

As secretary of state he was the logical choice for president in 1824. There was only one party at that time, the Democratic-Republicans, but factions had formed. As a result he ran against three other Republicans: Henry Clay, Andrew Jackson, and William H. Crawford. When no clear winner arose after the election, the House of Representatives chose Adams, who now had the support of Clay, his former opponent.

Improvements and Roadblocks

During his presidency Adams promoted the "American System," which placed tariffs on foreign goods and encouraged American manufacturers. He also established a national bank with a single currency and improved roads for transporting goods. Adams also proposed additional improvements, but since he refused to replace the pro-Jackson members of his administration—he believed that incompetence was the only cause for dismissal—Congress voted down many of his programs. He was able to extend the Cumberland Road in Ohio, begin construction on a number of new canals, and rebuild the Dismal Swamp Canal in North Carolina. The Erie Canal was also completed during his term.

"If your actions inspire others to dream more, learn more, do more and become more, you are a leader."

The unpopular Tariff of 1828, which steeply taxed foreign imports (called the Tariff of Abominations), ended Adams's chance of reelection; he lost in a landslide to Andrew Jackson. Adams expected to retire, but instead Massachusetts voters selected him as a member of the House of Representatives, where he served for 17 years. He argued against slavery, often managing to get around the "gag rule," which forbade any discussion of slavery.

In 1848 he suffered a cerebral hemorrhage and collapsed on the floor of the House. He died two days later and was buried in the family plot in Quincy.

BIOGRAPHICAL FACTS

Birth July 11, 1767, Braintree (now Quincy), Massachusetts

Religion Unitarian

Education Harvard University (graduated 1787)

Occupation Lawyer; politician

Other Offices Secretary to US minister to Russia; minister to the Netherlands; minister to Prussia; US senator; minister to Russia; peace commissioner at Treaty of Ghent; secretary of state; member of US House of Representatives

Political Party Democratic-Republican

Age at Inauguration 57

Vice President John C. Calhoun

Death February 23, 1848, Washington, DC

DID YOU KNOW...?

- John Quincy Adams was the first son of a president also elected president.
- Adams received an alligator as a gift from the Marquis de Lafayette. For a time the alligator resided in the bathroom of the East Room.
- For recreation, Adams enjoyed skinny-dipping in the Potomac River and playing billiards.

"Posterity: You will never know how much it has cost my generation to preserve your freedom. I hope you will make good use of it."

—John Quincy Adams

THE ADAMS FAMILY

Father John Adams (1735–1826)

Occupation Lawyer; politician; president

Mother Abigail Smith Adams (1744–1818)

Wife Louisa Catherine Johnson Adams

Birth February, 12, 1775, London, England

Marriage July 26, 1797

Death May 15, 1852, Washington, DC

Children George Washington (1801–1829); John (1803–1834); Charles Francis (1807–1886); Louisa Catherine (1811–1812)

Louisa Catherine Adams grew up in London, England, and Nantes, France. The couple married in London while John Adams was on a diplomatic mission.

Timeline of the Adams Presidency

US Events | **World Events**

1825 (World) Englishman William H. James designs a self-contained underwater breathing apparatus (SCUBA)

1825 (US) Henry Derringer produces the first of his small pistols, which become favorites of professional gamblers who could easily hide them

1825 (World) First wire suspension bridge opens near Lyon, France

1826 (World) London Zoo opens

1826 (US) The American Temperance Society forms in Boston with the goal to ban the sale and consumption of alcohol

1826 (US) Thomas Jefferson and John Adams die within hours of each other on the 50th anniversary of independence

1827 (World) English chemist John Walker invents the friction match

1827 (US) John James Audubon publishes Birds of America

1828 (World) Greeks win independence from the Ottoman Empire

1828 (US) "Tariff of Abominations," taxing imported goods and benefiting Northern industry, is passed

1827 (World) Joseph-Nicéphore Niépce of France takes the first photograph

Presidential Families

Children often want to follow in their parents' footsteps, and this has twice been the case with presidential sons. Once a presidential grandson followed his grandfather into the White House. Many presidents have been cousins—very remote cousins in some cases—of earlier presidents. Other presidents find themselves connected to their predecessors through marriage. There have also been a number of political dynasties in the United States, families boasting at least one president whose brothers, offspring, cousins, or spouses aspired to the office. Two of these, George Bush and Bill Clinton, have been in recent years. Even though it has been rare for a son to follow his father into the White House, the offspring of presidents frequently go into public service or hold political office.

The Harrisons

Benjamin Harrison of Ohio was the grandson of William Henry Harrison, a Virginian. Unlike his grandfather, who died after a month in office, Benjamin saw his term out. The two presidencies were separated by the terms of 13 other presidents.

Benjamin Harrison's daughter Mamie McKee and his daughter-in-law, Mary Harrison, with their children, Mary Lodge McKee, Marthena Harrison, and "Baby" McKee. The three babies could boast of a presidential grandfather and great-great-grandfather.

The Adamses

John Quincy Adams, son of the founding president John Adams, became the first presidential son to take the office of chief executive. John Quincy was also the first president to serve in Congress after his presidential term ended. One of his sons followed him into politics: Charles Francis was an ambassador and a member of the House.

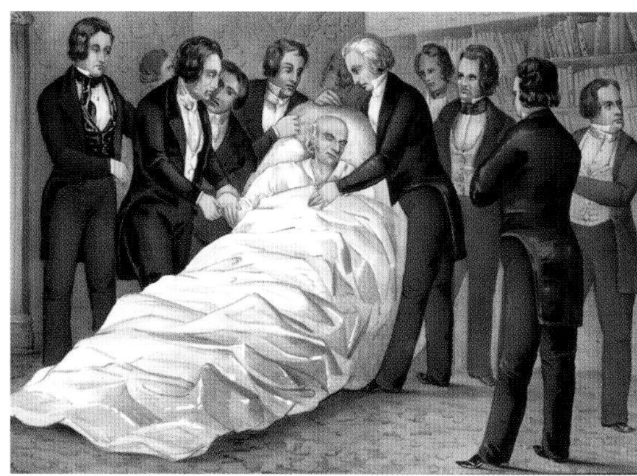

John Quincy Adams was a tireless public servant, working in Congress until he died—literally collapsing on the House floor.

The Roosevelts

When Franklin Delano Roosevelt of New York married Eleanor Roosevelt, a niece of Theodore Roosevelt, the 26th president, he became one of the most connected presidents in American history. FDR was also a fifth cousin of Theodore, and genealogists have determined that FDR was distantly related to at least 11 other US presidents, five by blood and six through marriage to Eleanor. His other connections include George Washington, the Adamses, James Madison, Martin Van Buren, the Harrisons, Zachary Taylor, Ulysses S. Grant, and William Howard Taft.

Eleanor Roosevelt on her wedding day in 1905. Her uncle Theodore gave her away. Franklin Roosevelt's marriage to Eleanor would add another six presidential connections to his list of five.

> "I want to avoid everything that is personal and I want it understood that I am grandson of nobody."
>
> —Benjamin Harrison

COUNT THE CONNECTIONS

Many presidents are related, some as close as father and son and others as only distant cousins. Here is a list of presidents with an estimated number of their presidential family ties:

George W. Bush	16
George H. W. Bush	16
William Howard Taft	14
Calvin Coolidge	14
Gerald R. Ford	14
Millard Fillmore	11
Franklin D. Roosevelt	11
Richard M. Nixon	10
Grover Cleveland	9
Herbert C. Hoover	9
Benjamin Harrison	8
John Quincy Adams	7
Rutherford B. Hayes	7
Ulysses S. Grant	6
Franklin Pierce	5
James A. Garfield	5
Warren G. Harding	5
John Adams	4
William Henry Harrison	4
Theodore Roosevelt	4
Jimmy Carter	4
George Washington	3
James Madison	2
Martin Van Buren	2
John Tyler	2
Zachary Taylor	2
Abraham Lincoln	2

The Bushes

Texan George Walker Bush, oldest son of George Herbert Walker Bush, was the second presidential son to be elected. As with the Adams presidents, father and son shared the same first name, and the sons were distinguished by middle name. George W.'s brother, Jeb, is also a politician who served as governor of Florida. Both George Bushes are related to 16 other presidents, including each other.

POLITICAL DYNASTIES

Some families with presidential aspirations form dynasties of sorts, with multiple generations in politics. Joseph Kennedy, a wealthy Massachusetts businessman and a US ambassador to Great Britain, groomed his sons from childhood to become leaders.

> **"Mothers all want their sons to grow up to be president, but they don't want them to become politicians in the process."**
>
> —John F. Kennedy

When the eldest son, Joseph Jr., died in World War II, John Fitzgerald Kennedy entered politics after serving in the war on a PT boat. In 1960, as a young senator from Massachusetts, he ran against the sitting vice president, Richard M. Nixon, and won, fulfilling his father's dream. After JFK's 1963 assassination, his brother Robert "Bobby" Kennedy, who had been JFK's attorney general, campaigned for the office. He too was assassinated, after giving a speech in Los Angeles. Youngest brother Senator Edward "Ted" Kennedy has been a Massachusetts senator for more than 40 years. His son Patrick is a multiterm congressman from Rhode Island.

Public office was also the career choice for two of Bobby's 11 kids: Kathleen Kennedy Townsend was lieutenant governor of Maryland, and Joseph Patrick Kennedy II was a member of the US House of Representatives. JFK's sister Eunice Kennedy Shriver also has political connections—her husband Sargent Shriver was an ambassador to France and candidate for vice president in 1972. Two of their children are also in the political realm: Mark Kennedy Shriver was a two-term delegate in the Maryland state legislature and Maria Shriver, as wife of Governor Arnold Schwarzenegger, is California's first lady.

Bobby, Eunice, Jean, Ted, and Pat Kennedy mob their brother John, lower right, and his new wife, Jacqueline, lower left, during the couple's wedding reception. The three Kennedy brothers all entered into politics.

Andrew Jackson

"Old Hickory"

1829–1837

Tall, hawk-faced Andrew Jackson was the first "frontier" president, and as such he worked for the good of the common people and helped shape the Democratic Party.

Jackson was born in Waxhaws, on the border of the two Carolinas, the son of poor Scots-Irish immigrants. In spite of a sparse education, he read law and became a prominent lawyer in Tennessee. He built his home, the Hermitage, outside Nashville, where he lived with his wife, Rachel Donelson Robards.

Tennessee chose Jackson as its first representative in Congress, and he also served in the Senate. He commanded the American forces in the Creek and Seminole wars and was the victor at the Battle of New Orleans in the War of 1812. His troops claimed he was "as tough as old hickory wood" on the battlefield and even called him "Old Hickory."

His popularity as a war hero gained him national recognition. After losing the presidential election to John Quincy Adams in 1824, Jackson won in 1828. Only the untimely death of his beloved wife shortly after his election marred this victory. To avoid corruption and patronage in his staff, President Jackson implemented a rotation of federal officeholders. He also reduced the national debt. After a financial depression, however, it grew ten times higher. Jackson battled to dismantle the Second Bank of the United States, which he felt concentrated too much wealth and power in one institution. In 1832 he succeeded, which led to the growth of local and state banks.

South Carolina Rebels

He also met with opposition from his vice president, John C. Calhoun, over the Tariff of 1828, which favored Northern industries over Southern planters. This led to the Nullification Crisis, when Calhoun's home state, South Carolina, claimed the right to void the tariff. Jackson declared the state was "on the brink of insurrection" and vowed to send troops to Charleston, South Carolina. Calhoun backed down and the tariff was lowered, but the incident foreshadowed the Civil War.

"The Constitution . . . forms a government not a league."

After Jackson won a second term with running mate, Martin Van Buren, two new parties evolved from the Democratic-Republican Party: the Democrats, favoring Jackson, and the National Republicans, or Whigs, who were against him.

Jackson's policy toward Native Americans, called the "Final Solution," involved removing the tribes to lands outside the borders of the American states. About 45,000 Indians were relocated, and thousands died in what has been called "one of the unhappiest chapters in American history."

At the end of his second term, he returned to the Hermitage, where he died of tuberculosis in 1845.

BIOGRAPHICAL FACTS

Birth March 15, 1767, Waxhaws, South Carolina

Religion Presbyterian

Education No formal education

Occupation Prosecutor; judge; planter; soldier

Other Offices Member of US House of Representatives; US senator; Tennessee Supreme Court justice; governor of the Florida Territory

Military Service Courier in American Revolution; major general of militia in Creek War; major general during War of 1812

Political Party Democratic-Republican

Vice President John C. Calhoun; Martin Van Buren

Age at Inauguration 61

Death June 8, 1845, Nashville, Tennessee

A 19th-century print made to celebrate General Jackson as the hero of the Battle of New Orleans during the War of 1812.

Rachel Jackson did not live to see her husband take office. She died soon after the election and was buried in the Hermitage garden wearing a dress bought for the inauguration. A grieving Jackson believed that slanderous campaign slurs helped bring about her death.

THE JACKSON FAMILY

Father Andrew Jackson (d. 1767)

Mother Elizabeth Hutchinson Jackson (d. 1781)

Wife Rachel Donelson Jackson

Birth June 15, 1767, Chatham, Virginia

Marriage January 7, 1794

Death December 22, 1828, Nashville, Tennessee

Adopted children Andrew Jackson Jr., Rachel's nephew (1808–1865); Lyncoya (1811–1828), a Creek Indian orphan; also guardian to eight other children

DID YOU KNOW . . . ?

- Jackson was possibly the first politician handed a baby to kiss. He politely passed the infant to his secretary of war.
- Jackson was wounded in so many duels, it was said he "rattled like a bag of marbles."
- After the death of Rachel, Jackson asked her niece Emily Donelson to act as White House hostess. She gave birth to three daughters while there.
- Jackson's critics called him "Jackass." His namesake animal later became the symbol of the Democratic Party.
- The $20 bill sports Jackson's image. Jackson has also appeared on $5, $10, $50, and $10,000 bills, as well as on a Confederate $1,000 bill.

Timeline of the Jackson Presidency

US Events	World Events
	1829 London's Metropolitan police, or "Bobbies," begin patrols
1830 Indian Removal Act is passed, forcing the emigration of tens of thousands of Indians	
	1830 Population of the world reaches one billion
1830 Religious visionary Joseph Smith founds the Church of Jesus Christ of Latter-day Saints (Mormons)	
	1831 French author Victor Hugo publishes *The Hunchback of Notre Dame*
1831 Virginia slave Nat Turner attempts a rebellion; more than 50 people are reported killed	
	1832 Michael Faraday of England builds the electric dynamo, or generator
	1834 British Empire abolishes slavery
	1834 Spanish Inquisition ends
1835 P. T. Barnum opens his first sideshow, exhibiting Joice Heth, who claimed to be the 161-year-old nurse to George Washington	
1836 Battle of the Alamo fought in mission in San Antonio, Texas	
	1837 British author Charles Dickens publishes *Oliver Twist*

8th President

Martin Van Buren

"Old Kinderhook"

1837–1841

Martin Van Buren guided the country through a period of great hardship and was an advocate of the Second Party System, which reshaped the politics and economy of the nation.

Born in 1782 to Dutch-speaking parents in Kinderhook, New York, Van Buren studied law in New York City. His father owned a tavern where political travelers often stopped, so Van Buren was drawn naturally into state politics. His ability to gain votes earned him a seat in the Senate in 1821. New Yorkers elected him as their governor in 1828, but he resigned from the office to take the position of Andrew Jackson's secretary of state.

An Influential Friend

A favorite of Jackson, who called him "a true man with no guile," the trim, well-dressed Van Buren was the president's most trusted advisor. He served as vice president under Jackson and was elected president in 1836. When he took office the country was prospering, but the Panic of 1837—caused by land speculation and inflationary practices by state banks—quickly changed that. Banks and businesses failed, thousands of Americans lost their land, and the country faced its greatest depression to date.

Difficult Times

Van Buren decided to retain Jackson's financial policies, an unpopular solution. When the Whigs recommended establishing a national bank to stabilize the economy, Van Buren resisted. Instead, he drastically reduced federal spending on internal improvements and opposed placing government funds in state banks, pushing for an independent treasury, which Congress authorized in 1840.

In 1837 Canadian rebels began using New York State as a base to attack Canada. When British forces crossed the border and attacked them, burning their ship the *Caroline*, one American was killed. Van Buren sent troops to destroy the rebel bases, even though many Americans sided with the rebel cause.

Van Buren riled Southerners by opposing the annexation of Texas, a potential slave state. His war on the Seminoles equally riled Northerners, who feared that it would lead to Florida being accepted as a slave state.

"As to the presidency, the two happiest days of my life were those of my entrance upon the office and my surrender of it."

When Van Buren ran for a second term, the Whigs portrayed their candidate William Henry Harrison as a tough, capable soldier, the opposite of the refined Van Buren. Harrison won, and although Van Buren ran for president several more times, most notably for the anti-slavery Free Soil Party, the White House eluded him.

After a two-year trip to Europe, Van Buren died at Lindenwald, his estate near Kinderhook, in 1862.

BIOGRAPHICAL FACTS

Birth December 5, 1782, Kinderhook, New York

Religion Dutch Reformed

Education Kinderhook Academy

Occupation Lawyer

Other Offices New York state senator; New York attorney-general; US senator; governor of New York; secretary of state; minister to England; vice president

Political Party Democratic

Vice President Richard Mentor Johnson

Age at Inauguration 55

Death July 24, 1862, Kinderhook, New York

Van Buren ran again for president. Shown here is a campaign banner for the presidential race of 1848. Van Buren's running mate in the unsuccessful try was Charles Francis Adams, son of John Quincy.

"Bless our beloved country with honors and with length of days. May her ways be ways of pleasantness and all her paths be peace!"

—Martin Van Buren

DID YOU KNOW . . . ?

- Van Buren was the first president born a US citizen.
- Van Buren spoke Dutch as a child, making him the first president who learned English as a second language.
- Van Buren's supporters shortened "Old Kinderhook" to "OK," which may have led to the slang term used today for "all right."

Father Abraham Van Buren (1737–1817)

Occupation Tavern keeper

Mother Maria Hoes Van Buren (1747–1818)

Wife Hannah Hoes Van Buren

Birth March 8, 1783, Kinderhook, New York

Marriage February 21, 1807

Death February 5, 1819, New York, New York

Children Abraham (1807–1873); John (1810–1866); Martin (1812–1855); Winfield Scott (1813); Smith Thompson (1817–1876)

Van Buren's wife, Hannah, had died many years before his presidency, but his daughter-in-law, Angelica Singleton Van Buren, shown here, was an eager fill-in as White hostess. Known for her extravagant sense of style, Angelica was also well connected. Her friend and mentor, former first lady Dolley Madison, had introduced her to the president's oldest son, Abraham.

Timeline of the Van Buren Presidency

US Events | **World Events**

1837 (US) Michigan admitted to the Union

1837 (World) Victoria is crowned queen of England, heralding the start of the 64-year Victorian era

1837 (World) *Caroline* Affair creates hostility with Canada and Britain

1837 (US) Samuel Morse demonstrates the electric telegraph

1838 (World) German-English engineer Augustus Siebe invents closed diving suit with helmet

1838 (US) The removal of the Cherokee from their ancestral home in a forced march results in "Trail of Tears," which killed about 4,000 people

1839 (US) Charles Goodyear invents the vulcanizing process for curing rubber

1840 (World) Edgar Allan Poe publishes *Tales of the Grotesque*

1840 (World) German chemist Justus von Liebig invents artificial fertilizer

1840 (World) Antoine Joseph Sax invents the saxophone and patents it six years later

1840 (World) Duchess of Bedford introduces afternoon tea to Britain

1840 (US) 90 percent of the US population lives in rural areas

William Henry Harrison

"Old Tippecanoe" **1841**

9th President

Although portrayed in political campaigns as a hard-drinking soldier, William Henry Harrison was in reality the aristocratic son of a Virginia planter. His fame as a war hero led to his election, but illness cut short his presidency.

Early Career

Harrison was born at Berkeley Plantation in 1773. After graduating from Hampden-Sydney College he began to study medicine, but a craving for adventure led him to buy a commission in the army. Stationed in the Northwest, he campaigned against the American Indians with General "Mad Anthony" Wayne. Harrison fought at the critical Battle of Fallen Timbers, which resulted in the opening up of the Ohio Territory.

In 1798 Harrison became secretary of the Northwest Territory, and he served as its first delegate to Congress. He also served for 12 years as governor of the Indiana Territory, where it was his responsibility to protect settlements from Indian raids. In 1809, when two Shawnee brothers, Tecumseh and Tenskwatawa (the Prophet), began stirring up the tribes, Harrison received permission to attack their forces. His troops, who greatly outnumbered the Indian forces, put down the uprising at the famous Battle of Tippecanoe. Still, the nation hailed Harrison as a hero.

"I contend that the strongest of all governments is that which is most free."

In the War of 1812 Harrison continued to earn military honors, and he was made brigadier general of the Army of the Northwest. In the decisive Battle of the Thames, near Lake Erie in Canada, he defeated British and Indian forces. Tecumseh was killed in the battle, and the Indians were never again a serious threat in that area.

A Fateful Inauguration

In 1840 the Whigs nominated Harrison to run for president against Martin Van Buren. His margin in the popular vote was slight, but he easily won the electoral college. Always impressed with the classics, Harrison penned a long-winded inaugural speech. He asked Secretary of State Daniel Webster to edit it. Webster, after removing many classical references, later commented that he killed "seventeen Roman proconsuls as dead as smelts, every one of them."

But the speech remained lengthy, and when Harrison delivered it—on one of the coldest days the capital had seen—the tough old soldier refused to wear an overcoat or hat. Within weeks he fell ill with a cold that turned to viral pneumonia. Doctors vainly tried every kind of cure on the ailing president, including Indian remedies. On April 4, 1841, he died, having served exactly one month.

BIOGRAPHICAL FACTS

Birth February 9, 1773, Berkeley Plantation, Virginia

Religion Episcopalian

Education Hampden-Sydney College; University of Pennsylvania

Other Offices Secretary of Northwest Territory; territorial delegate to Congress; governor of the Indiana Territory; member of the US House of Representatives; US senator; minister to Colombia

Military Service Ensign First Infantry Regiment, left as captain; major general Northwest Army

Political Party Whig

Vice President John Tyler

Age at Inauguration 68

Death April 4, 1841, Washington, DC

A print of William Henry Harrison by Currier & Ives, a 19th-century printmaking firm that specialized in inexpensive, popular images.

The "log cabin" presidential campaign of 1840 portrayed Harrison as just a "regular guy." This image shows him in front of a log cabin, inviting two soldiers to enjoy some hard cider. The flag bears the names "Harrison & Tyler." John Tyler was Harrison's running mate in the election, which led to the slogan "Tippecanoe and Tyler too."

"Some folks are silly enough to have formed a plan to make a President of the US out of this Clerk and Clod hopper."

—William Henry Harrison

THE HARRISON FAMILY

Father Benjamin Harrison (1726–1791)

Occupation Planter

Mother Elizabeth Bassett Harrison (1730–1792)

Wife Anna Tuthill Symmes

Birth July 25, 1775, Flatbrook, New Jersey

Marriage November 25, 1795

Death February, 25, 1864, Morristown, New Jersey

Children Elizabeth Bassett (1796–1846); John Cleves Symmes (1798–1830); Lucy Singleton (1800–1826); William Henry (1802–1838); John Scott (1806–1840); Mary Symmes (1809–1842); Carter Bassett (1811–1839); Anna Tuthill (1813–1865); James Findlay (1814–1817)

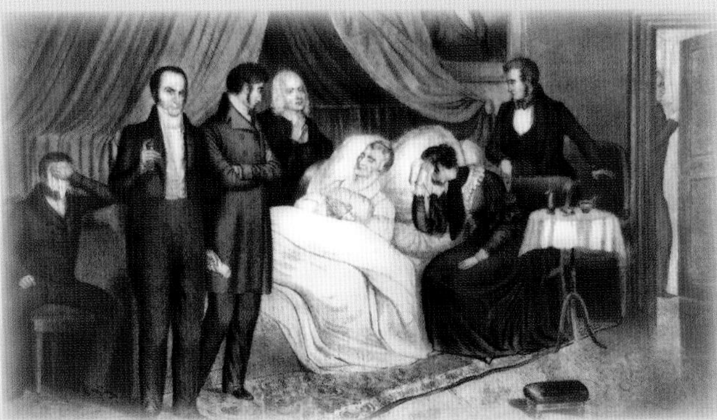

A 19th-century print depicts Harrison's family and friends gathering around the deathly ill president. Harrison was the first president to die in office. He also served the shortest term and gave the longest inaugural speech.

Timeline of the Harrison Presidency

US Events | **World Events**

1841 (US) The first continuous filibuster, an attempt to impede voting by obstructive tactics, such as making long speeches, lasts nearly a month in the Senate

1841 (World) Edgar Allen Poe publishes *The Murders in the Rue Morgue*, considered the first detective story

1841 (US) Napoleon Guerin of New York City patents a life preserver made of cork

1841 (World) New Zealand made a British colony

1841 (US) The first US steam fire engine is tested in New York City

1841 (World) Scots physician James Baird discovers hypnosis

1841 (US) Samuel Slocum patents the stapler

1841 (US) The first emigrant wagon train leaves Independence, Missouri, for California

1841 (World) Upper Canada and Lower Canada united

1841–1869 (US) Approximately 400,000 settlers cross the American West on the Oregon Trail

1841 (World) Thomas Cook opens the first travel agency

Presidents of a Nation in Conflict

The Battle of Chantilly, on September 1, 1862, in Fairfax County, Virginia. Although this was the last battle of the Northern Virginia campaign, the bitter war between the North and South would rage on for nearly three more years. The Civil War claimed more than 600,000 American lives.

In his autobiography Thomas Jefferson wrote of slavery: "Nothing is more certainly written in the book of fate than that these people are to be free." Perhaps he understood that the slavery question would one day divide the nation and ultimately lead it to a civil war. The events leading up to this war, its grim reality, and its uneasy aftermath put enormous strain on the country, and on the presidents who had to cope with its challenges.

"It is well that war is so terrible, or we should grow too fond of it."

—Robert E. Lee

Historians agree that the Civil War had many causes—the battle for states' rights, the needs of Northern industries versus Southern plantations, and the election of Northerner Abraham Lincoln—but slavery was at the heart of most of them.

Slavery began in the colonies around 1620, when Africans were shipped to the Americas to work the South's large tobacco and indigo plantations. With the advent of cotton as a cash crop, the demand for slaves increased. By 1860 the 15 slaveholding states claimed more than four million slaves—one-quarter of their total population.

As territories entered the Union, the question of whether they would become free states or slave states became critical to the balance of power.

With their economy so closely tied to slavery, Southern politicians fought for creating more slave states, even outside of the South. They reasoned that the more slave states there were, the less chance of the practice being abolished.

During James Monroe's term, the Missouri Compromise admitted Missouri as a slave state and Maine as free and prohibited slavery to the west and north of Missouri. In 1854 Franklin Pierce was pressured to sign the Kansas-Nebraska Act, which revoked these restrictions. When Kansas declared as a free territory, militant pro-slavery factions entered Kansas. Fighting broke out between them and the anti-slavery forces, leading to hostilities that lasted through the mid and late 1850s. A New York newspaper editor described the violence as "Bleeding Kansas."

A strong abolitionist movement of women and men worked to end slavery, which the Northern states had already outlawed. Some abolitionists relied on legislation; others took up arms, such as John Brown, who raided the US Armory and Arsenal at Harpers Ferry, Virginia, hoping to inspire a slave rebellion. Seven men died in the raid, Brown was tried and hanged, and the nation was further split on the slavery issue. Abolitionists secretly formed the "Underground Railroad" to smuggle escaped slaves out of the country. Former slave Harriet Tubman was one of its most famous "conductors."

The Civil War Begins

Shortly after Abraham Lincoln's election in 1860, South Carolina broke away from the Union, followed by Mississippi, Florida, Alabama, Georgia, Louisiana, Texas, Virginia, Arkansas, Tennessee, and North Carolina. In February 1861 the Confederate States of America formed. The nation was now officially divided.

During this bitter conflict, which lasted until 1865, more than 600,000 Confederate and Union soldiers died in battle or of disease. In 1862 Abraham Lincoln issued the Emancipation Proclamation, freeing slaves in any states held by the Confederacy, hoping to weaken the South from within. After the surrender of General Robert E. Lee, the commander of the Southern army, to Union general Ulysses S. Grant, Grant advised Lincoln to take a liberal course when reconstructing the economically shattered South. But Lincoln's assassination put the rebuilding of the South in the hands of Radical Republicans, who chose harsher measures over leniency. Military rule was instituted in the former Confederate states until 1876, when Rutherford B. Hayes officially ended Reconstruction.

Without slave labor, Southern plantations were much less profitable, but Northern industry expanded. The South's resentment against the victors grew, and it took the country decades to move on. But move on it did, eventually becoming a stronger nation. The Civil War served as a reminder to all Americans that the needs of individual states were ultimately less important than keeping the United States truly united.

WHAT DOES THAT MEAN?

Abolitionism A movement to end slavery
Copperheads Northern Democrats who opposed the Civil War and wanted a peace settlement with the Confederates
Emancipation Freeing a person or a people
Radical Republicans The pro-war, anti-slavery faction of the Republican Party
Reconstruction The rebuilding of the former Confederate states after the Civil War
Sectionalism Politically favoring one geographic area over another

JEFFERSON DAVIS

The Confederate States of America had but one president: Jefferson Davis (1808–1889). Like many Southerners who took up arms against the North, Davis was a graduate of West Point. He then served as second in command to Zachary Taylor during the Black Hawk War. While in this role, Davis met and fell in love with Taylor's daughter Sarah Knox. Taylor would only approve a marriage between them if Davis left the military: life at army posts was too hard. Davis complied, but, tragically, Sarah died only three months after the June 1835 wedding.

John Tyler

"His Accidency"

1841–1845

John Tyler at first strengthened the role of the president. Yet his term saw the pro- and anti-slavery movements begin to polarize the country.

The "Accidental" President

Tyler was born in Charles City County, Virginia, and his father was a future governor of that state. Tyler attended the College of William and Mary to study law. At age 26 he was already a member of the House of Representatives. There he opposed the Missouri Compromise, which dictated slavery policies of future states. Virginians elected him governor in 1825, and he also served in the US Senate from 1827 to 1836.

The Whig Party chose him as running mate for war hero William Henry Harrison in 1840. Upon the death of President Harrison, Tyler became the first American vice president to step into his predecessor's role. Tyler claimed the full powers of an elected president. He took the oath of office and continued his term with the approval of Congress, although some opponents called him the "acting president" or "His Accidency."

Tyler's first wife, Letitia, was a pretty but fragile woman. She spent her days with family on the second floor of the White House, unable to act as hostess. On September 10, 1842, she became the first president's wife to die in the mansion.

Angering the Whigs

The new president quickly found himself in trouble with his Whig supporters when he vetoed most of their bills, especially those of powerful Henry Clay, who was pushing for a national bank. In 1842 Tyler did sign a tariff bill protecting Northern manufacturers. But with the government virtually stalled, the Whigs expelled Tyler from the party.

"I can never consent to being dictated to."

He named Southerner and former Whig John C. Calhoun secretary of state in 1844, further angering the Whigs. By the end of Tyler's term, Southern conservatives made up his cabinet. The sectional, or regional, politics that would soon tear the country apart—Southern Democrats favoring planters and Northern Whigs supporting manufacturing—had started to evolve.

Tyler worked for the annexation of Texas, and his term saw the passing of the "Log Cabin" bill, which allowed settlers the right to claim 160 acres of land before it was put up for public sale. He also survived an impeachment investigation.

After he left office, Tyler chaired the Virginia Peace Convention, and in 1861 he served in the Confederate Congress. He remained a slaveholder all of his life. He died of bronchitis in 1862—with the country engaged in a civil war.

BIOGRAPHICAL FACTS

Birth March 29, 1790, Charles City County, Virginia

Religion Episcopalian

Education College of William and Mary (graduated 1807)

Occupation Lawyer

Other Offices Virginia House of Delegates; member of US House of Representatives; Virginia State legislator; governor of Virginia; US senator; vice president; member of Confederate States Congress

Political Party Whig

Vice President None

Age at Inauguration 51

Death January 18, 1862, Richmond, Virginia

Sheet music for "Hail to the Chief," the US president's anthem. Julia Tyler, Tyler's second wife, suggested that a band strike up the tune when a president made an appearance.

DID YOU KNOW . . . ?

- Tyler's favorite horse was named The General and is buried at his Sherwood Forest Plantation.
- Tyler loved to play the violin.
- Tyler was the great-uncle of future president Harry S. Truman.

A TRAGIC ACCIDENT

Before her marriage to Tyler, Julia Gardiner, her father, and her sister joined the president for a cruise on the Potomac aboard the USS *Princeton*. Thomas Gardiner, as well as the secretary of the navy and the secretary of state, was among those killed when a huge naval gun exploded. Julia fainted into the president's arms.

THE TYLER FAMILY

Father John Tyler (1747–1813)

Occupation Planter; politician

Mother Mary Armistead (1761–1797)

First Wife Letitia Christian Tyler (1790–1842)

Marriage March 29, 1813

Children Mary (1815–1848); Robert (1816–1877); John (1819–1896); Letitia (1821–1907); Elizabeth (1823–1850); Anne Contesse (1825); Alice (1827–1854); Tazewell (1830–1874)

Tyler's first wife, Letitia, suffered a stroke during her husband's term.

Second Wife Julia Gardiner Tyler (1820–1889)

Marriage June 26, 1844

Children David Gardiner (1846–1927); John Alexander (1848–1883); Julia Gardiner (1849–1871); Lachlan (1851–1902); Lyon Gardiner (1853–1935); Robert Fitzwalter (1856–1927); Pearl (1860–1947)

Timeline of the Tyler Presidency

US Events | **World Events**

1842 (US)
A ten-hour workday established for Massachusetts children under age 12

1841 (World)
Scots physician James Baird discovers hypnosis

1843 (US)
Patent issued to Nancy Johnson for hand-cranked ice cream maker

1843 (World)
Alexander Bain of Scotland invents an early fax machine

1843 (US)
W. & S. B. Ives publishes the first commercially produced American board game, called the Mansion of Happiness

1843 (World)
Henry Cole pioneers the Christmas card

1844 (World)
The first YMCA opens in London, England

1844 (US)
Samuel F. B. Morse sends the first public telegraph message.

1844 (US)
Wells, Fargo & Co. founded

1844 (World)
French author Alexandre Dumas publishes *The Three Musketeers*

1845 (US)
Texas annexation leads to war with Mexico

James K. Polk

"Young Hickory"

1845–1849

James K. Polk was an advocate of national expansion. The last strong president until Lincoln, he set a four-year agenda—and kept it.

Born in Mecklenburg County, North Carolina, Polk grew up in Nashville, Tennessee. He attended the University of North Carolina, graduating with honors. While serving in the Tennessee Legislature, he married Sarah Childress, an intelligent, well-read young woman, who had attended the Moravian "female academy" in North Carolina (now Salem College), one of the very few institutions of higher learning then available to women.

During Polk's time in the legislature, Andrew Jackson befriended him. This was a lasting connection that would alter Polk's political career. After serving in the House, where he was Speaker from 1835 to 1837, Polk was chosen governor of Tennessee. Later, as a potential vice presidential candidate, Polk began campaigning on a platform of annexing Texas and securing Oregon, two things the presidential candidates refused to discuss. Jackson, who approved of expansionism, urged Polk's nomination for president at the Democratic Convention. When voters elected him in 1844, his surprised opponents asked, "Who is Polk?"

Setting Boundaries

Both agendas the new president supported risked the outbreak of war—with Mexico over Texas and with England over Oregon. In Oregon the Democrats wanted the border with Canada to be at latitude 54°40′, just south of Russian-held Alaska. This led to the slogan "Fifty-four forty or fight!" Polk reached a compromise with England and the border was set at the 49th parallel from the Rockies west.

Polk's purchase of California proved more difficult. Polk offered $20 million for California and the New Mexico Territory, but the Mexican government refused to negotiate. Polk then sent General Zachary Taylor to patrol the Rio Grande, and the angered Mexicans attacked. In spite of Northern opposition, Congress declared war. In 1848, after a number of American victories, Mexico finally ceded the territories to the United States. The new lands were valuable additions to the country—comparable to the Louisiana Purchase—but the issues they raised over whether they would enter as "free" or as "slave" territories continued to divide the North and South.

"With me it is exceptionally true that the Presidency is no bed of roses."

His term of office was hard on the president's health, and Polk died shortly after his retirement to his home, Polk Place, in Nashville, Tennessee. His last words were to his beloved wife: "I love you, Sarah. For all eternity, I love you."

11th President

BIOGRAPHICAL FACTS

Birth November 2, 1795, Pineville, North Carolina

Religion Presbyterian/Methodist

Education University of North Carolina (graduated summa cum laude, 1818)

Occupation Planter; lawyer

Other Offices Member of Tennessee House of Representatives; member of US House of Representatives; Speaker of the House; governor of Tennessee

Political Party Democratic

Vice President George M. Dallas

Age at Inauguration 49

Death June 15, 1849, Nashville, Tennessee

Although his term has been called "the one bright spot in the dull void between Jackson and Lincoln," Polk remains one of the little-known presidents.

The Polk marriage was a true partnership that ended at the sudden death of James just months after his retirement to Polk Place in Tennessee. Sarah wore only widow's black for the remaining 42 years of her life.

DID YOU KNOW . . . ?

- A political protégé of "Old Hickory" Andrew Jackson, Polk became known as "Young Hickory."
- Polk was a slaveholder and owned a cotton plantation until his death.
- In 1848 Polk offered an astounding $100 million for Cuba. Spain rejected it.
- Sarah Polk helped write her husband's speeches, advised him on policy matters, and assisted in his campaigns.

THE POLK FAMILY

Father Samuel Polk (1772–1827)

Occupation Planter

Mother Jane Knox Polk (1776–1852)

Wife Sarah Childress Polk

Marriage January 1, 1824

Birth September 4, 1803, Murfreesboro, Tennessee

Death August 14, 1891, Nashville, Tennessee

Children None

"Wealthy, pretty, ambitious, and intelligent."

—Andrew Jackson, about Sarah Polk

Timeline of the Polk Presidency

US Events / **World Events**

1845 (US) Florida and Texas admitted to the Union

1845 (World) Scotsman Robert Thomson invents pneumatic tire

1846 (US) Smithsonian Institution founded

1846 (World) Elias Howe invents sewing machine

1846 (US) Iowa admitted to the Union

1846 (US) A large crack appears in the Liberty Bell

1847 (World) Famous jewelry store Cartier opens in Paris

1847 (US) Hanson Crockett Gregory, age 15, of Camden, Maine, invents the ring doughnut

1847 (World) British Museum opens

1847 (World) In Britain, James Simpson uses chloroform to ease pain of childbirth

1848 (US) Gold discovered at Sutter's Mill in Coloma, California

1848 (World) Marx and Engels publish the *Communist Manifesto*

1848 (US) Wisconsin admitted to the Union

Zachary Taylor

"Old Rough and Ready" **1849–1850**

Zachary Taylor was another war hero president, even though he hadn't held a single political office prior to his election to the nation's highest position. But like the hardened soldier he was, Taylor battled to hold the Union together.

Born in Orange County, Virginia, and raised on a plantation in Kentucky, Taylor had little schooling when he embarked on a military career. He had settled in Baton Rouge, Louisiana, and owned a plantation in Mississippi, but he spent 25 years at various frontier outposts battling Indians. He was then sent to fight the forces of Mexico.

Taylor had gained the nickname "Old Rough and Ready" for his rumpled appearance. President Polk, displeased with Taylor's informality and his Whig ties, chose to send General Winfield Scott to capture Mexico City. Taylor countered with a stunning victory at the Battle of Buena Vista—even though his troops were outnumbered four to one.

After his successful campaign in the Mexican War, the Whigs nominated him for president. As a slaveholder, they reasoned, he would attract Southern voters, and his war record and homespun manner would attract Northerners. The Northerners were not swayed by his down-to-earth charm and formed the anti-slavery Free Soil Party led by former president Martin Van Buren.

Standing Firm

Taylor narrowly won the election—and was the last Southerner elected president until Woodrow Wilson in 1912. In spite of his lack of political expertise, Taylor was not content to let his party dictate policy. His years in the army had also given him a strong nationalist streak. When he encouraged New Mexico and California to draw up constitutions and apply for statehood, the angry Southerners feared that the former territories would not declare for slavery. Congress was furious and felt that he had taken away its right to decide on slavery for new territories.

> **"The idea that I should become President . . . has never entered my head, nor is it likely to enter the head of any other person."**

When Southern leaders threatened to secede from the Union, Taylor vowed to lead the army against them, declaring that he would hang anyone "taken in rebellion against the Union."

Taylor died unexpectedly, after a sudden stomach illness, in the summer of 1850. He had just attended a July 4th celebration at the Washington Monument, and the city's extreme heat, or possibly some tainted cherries, was blamed for his death.

His presidential term was short, but Zachary Taylor, who knew too well the costs of battle, had managed to hold back the war clouds that were looming ever closer on the horizon.

BIOGRAPHICAL FACTS

Birth November 24, 1784, Orange County, Virginia
Religion Episcopalian
Education No formal education
Occupation Planter; soldier
Military Service First lieutenant of infantry, 1808, resigned as major general, 1848
Political Party Whig
Vice President Millard Fillmore
Age at Inauguration 64
Death July 9, 1850, Washington, DC

His war hero reputation made Taylor popular with the public. Companies even used his image and name to promote their products, such as Rough & Ready Twist tobacco.

DID YOU KNOW...?

Pictures of Zachary Taylor often showed him with his favorite horse, Old Whitey.

- Taylor studied to become a teacher at the urging of his future wife.
- Margaret Taylor traveled with her soldier husband and shared the hardships of frontier life.
- Taylor's funeral procession included his favorite horse, Old Whitey, parading with an empty saddle and inverted spurs.
- He was a descendant of King Edward I of England.
- Taylor's body was exhumed in 1991 and tested negative for arsenic poisoning.

THE TAYLOR FAMILY

Father Richard Taylor (d. 1829)
Occupation Soldier
Mother Sarah Dabney Strother Taylor (1760–1822)
Wife Margaret Mackall Smith Taylor
Marriage June 21, 1810
Birth September 21, 1788, Calvert County, Maryland
Death August 14, 1852, Pascagoula, Mississippi

Children Ann Mackall (1811–1875); Sarah Knox (1814–1835); Octavia (1816–1820); Margaret Smith (1819–1820); Mary Elizabeth (1824–1909); Richard (1826–1879)

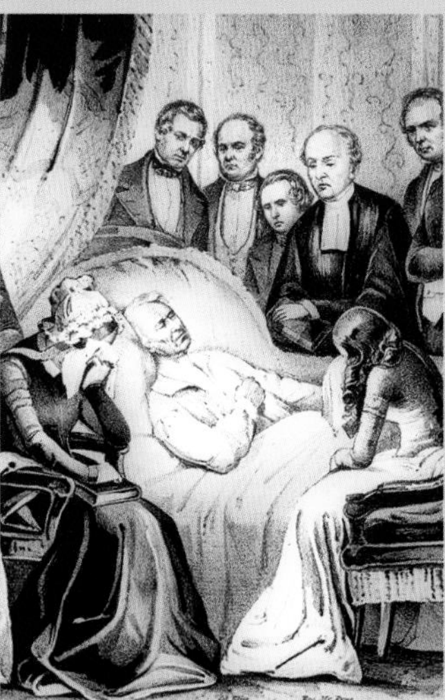

Family and friends gather at the president's bedside to make their final good-byes.

Timeline of the Taylor Presidency

US Events | **World Events**

1849 (World) The bowler hat, or derby, is invented in Britain

1849 (US) Walter Hunt invents the safety pin

1849 (World) Hungary declares independence from Austria

1850–1870 (US) Plains Indians cede land in exchange for reservations

1850 (World) Clayton-Bulwer Treaty with Great Britain guarantees that any canal across Central America would be available to all nations

1850 (US) Nathaniel Hawthorne publishes *The Scarlet Letter*

1850 (US) Woman's Medical College of Pennsylvania opens as the first female medical school.

1850 (US) First year of the Pinkerton Detective Agency, which uses a picture of a eye with the words "We Never Sleep"

1850 (World) Armand Hippolyte Fizeau determines the approximate speed of light

1850 (US) California is admitted to the Union

1850 (US) Levi Strauss & Co., maker of blue jeans, is founded

The Houses of Congress

The United States Congress makes up the legislative—or lawmaking—branch of the federal government.

It consists of two houses: the Senate and the House of Representatives. Senators and representatives are chosen by direct election and meet in Washington in the US Capitol.

The Constitution grants Congress the power to collect taxes, oversee federal spending, borrow money, regulate both foreign and domestic commerce, and coin money. Congress has the power to declare war, suppress invasions or insurrections, and raise the armed forces. It can establish post offices and courts lower than the Supreme Court and issue patents and copyrights. As an instrument of checks and balances, Congress oversees the executive branch, usually through a committee consisting of members from both houses. Congress has presided over several presidential impeachments. Congress is also responsible for approving the admission of new states and territories.

To handle situations not specified in the Constitution, Congress also possesses an "implied" power to "make all laws which shall be necessary and proper for carrying into execution the foregoing powers."

Two Chambers under One Roof

The two houses evolved from the Continental Congress, which was made up of delegates from the 13 original states. While attending the Constitutional Convention, James Madison suggested a bicameral, or two-part, congress, with the lower house delegates being elected by the people, and the upper house delegates being chosen by members of the lower house. Smaller states favored one congress with equal representation for all states, regardless of size. A compromise was reached, with each state having only two senators but multiple representatives based on population. Having two houses of legislation would also allow for checks and balances to prevent misuse of power by either house.

The inside of the Capitol dome is as impressive as the outside. Looking up in the Rotunda reveals its sunlit windows and colorful paintings.

The Senate

Each state is allowed two senators, who are elected for six-year terms. There are no term limitations on senators, and many have served for decades. The Senate has frequently served as a stepping-stone to the White House—many voters believe that experience with Washington insider politics gives a presidential candidate an advantage.

The House of Representatives

The number of representatives for each state is based on its population. Large, sparsely settled states may have fewer representatives than small, heavily populated states. Representatives serve two-year terms. The leader of the house is called the Speaker and is the second person in line for the presidency, after the vice president.

HOW LAWS ARE MADE

Laws can be introduced in either house of Congress. When a legislator has an idea for a law or bill, he or she is called the sponsor. The idea is placed in a box called the "hopper," and a clerk assigns it a number and a designation: "H. R." for House of Representatives and "S." for Senate. The bill is printed and distributed to the members of Congress to review. It is then assigned to a committee, which will study it. Releasing the bill for voting is "reporting it out," while setting it aside is "tabling it." If a bill passes in the House—usually after a debate—it then moves to the Senate. If the Senate approves the bill, it then goes to the president, who has ten days to either sign it into law or veto it. In case of a veto, both the Senate and the House must approve the bill by a two-thirds vote, in which case it passes and becomes an act.

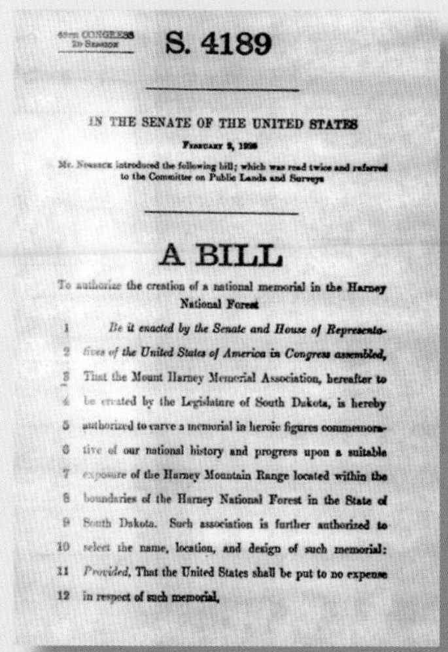

S. 4189

IN THE SENATE OF THE UNITED STATES

Mr. [illegible] introduced the following bill; which was read twice and referred to the Committee on Public Lands and Surveys

A BILL

To authorize the creation of a national memorial in the Harney National Forest

Be it enacted by the Senate and House of Representatives of the United States of America in Congress assembled, That the Mount Harney Memorial Association, hereafter to be created by the Legislature of South Dakota, is hereby authorized to carve a memorial in heroic figures commemorative of our national history and progress upon a suitable exposure of the Harney Mountain Range located within the boundaries of the Harney National Forest in the State of South Dakota. Such association is further authorized to select the name, location, and design of such memorial: *Provided,* That the United States shall be put to no expense in respect of such memorial,

A Senate bill from the 1920s, marked with an "S." just as bills are today.

The Capitol Building

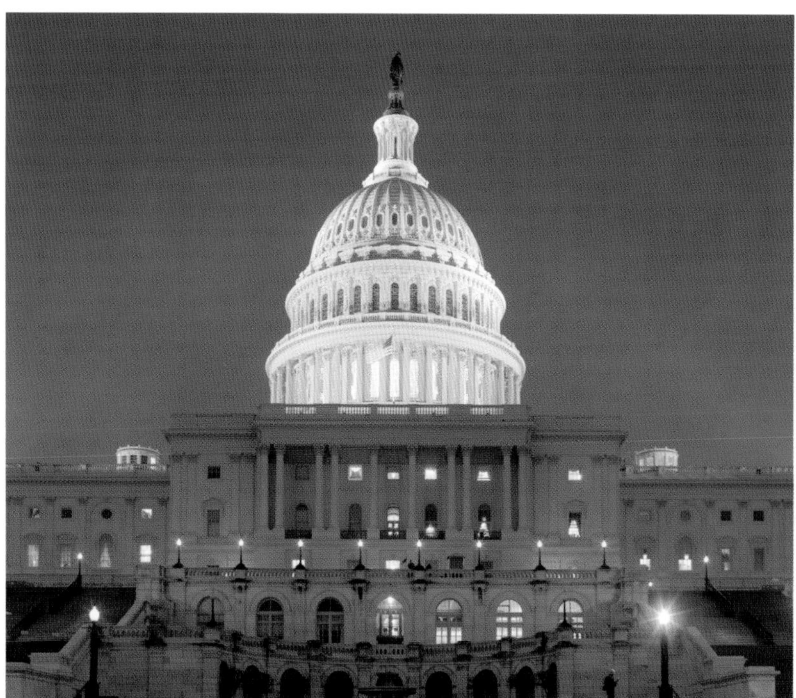

The Capitol in Washington, DC, sits on top of Capitol Hill at the east end of the National Mall.

With its impressive dome, the United States Capitol is a noted symbol of the nation. For more than 200 years Congress has met in its halls to legislate the laws of the land.

The Capitol's History

Like the White House, the Capitol was designed by the winner of a competition, in this case Dr. William Thornton. President Washington laid the cornerstone in September 1793. From 1855 to 1866 the building underwent a major reconstruction. African Americans—free and slave—completed most of the work.

The Capitol Today

Today the Capitol has two distinct wings, one for each chamber of Congress: the north contains the Senate and the south contains the House of Representatives. Above both chambers are galleries where visitors can watch senators and representatives in action.

The central portion of the building features the Rotunda, the great hall beneath the dome. It is used for ceremonies, such as inaugurations and the lying in state of presidents. Beneath the Rotunda lies the Crypt. Despite its eerie name, no one is buried there—the space is used instead as a gallery. Inside the dome itself are paintings of significant events in US history. Atop the dome, on the outside, stands the Statue of Freedom.

The Capitol Grounds

The grounds include terraces, gardens, and the famous staircases. Each wing has a flagpole on top: if a flag is flying over the north wing, that means the Senate below is in session. If there is one over the south, the House is in session.

13th President

Millard Fillmore

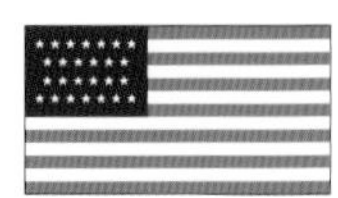

"The American Louis-Philippe" **1850–1853**

Though not a brilliant politician, Millard Fillmore was an amiable man and avid reader who rose from a log cabin to the White House.

Humble Beginnings

Born into hardship, Fillmore grew up on a farm in New York's Finger Lake region. While attending a one-room schoolhouse as a young man, he fell in love with the redheaded teacher, Abigail Powers, and later married her. He was admitted to the bar in 1823 and seven years later moved his law practice to Buffalo. He then served in the House of Representatives for eight years. While comptroller of New York, he was chosen as running mate for Zachary Taylor, whom he had never met.

As vice president, Fillmore presided over the Senate during the critical debates on Henry Clay's Compromise of 1850, which was meant to address the territorial and slavery controversies that arose after the Mexican-American War. Though he did not voice his own opinion of slavery, Fillmore believed that the Southern economy would fail without it. When Taylor died in office, the cabinet resigned. New President Fillmore appointed pro-Compromise Daniel Webster, a moderate Whig, as secretary of state. When Clay became ill, it fell to Webster and Senator Stephen A. Douglas of Illinois to lead the fight for the Compromise.

The Senate Casts Its Vote

President Fillmore now came out in support of the Compromise. To help make it more acceptable to Congress, Senator Douglas broke it up into five separate bills:

1. Admit California as a free state.
2. Settle the Texas boundary and compensate Texas for the loss of New Mexico lands.
3. Grant territorial status to New Mexico.
4. Place federal officers at the disposal of slaveholders seeking fugitives.
5. Abolish the slave trade in the District of Columbia.

The Senate passed all five bills, but the Northern states were angered that Fillmore had signed the Fugitive Slave Act, which allowed runaway slaves to be captured and returned to their owners.

"May God save the country, for it is evident that the people will not."

Fillmore always desired to keep the status quo, and he felt his success with the Compromise would ease national tensions over slavery. But it was only a patch on a very large crack that was threatening to split the country apart.

Fillmore was not renominated, but ran again as candidate for the Know-Nothing Party in 1856 and lost. He vocally opposed Lincoln's policies during the Civil War.

BIOGRAPHICAL FACTS

Birth January 7, 1800, Locke Township, New York

Religion Unitarian

Education No formal education

Occupation Prosecutor; judge; planter; soldier

Other Offices Member of New York State Assembly; member of US House of Representatives; comptroller of New York; vice president

Political Party Whig; Know-Nothing

Vice President John C. Calhoun; Martin Van Buren

Age at Inauguration 50

Death March 8, 1874, Buffalo, New York

Campaign banner from the 1848 election showing running mates Zachary Taylor and Millard Fillmore. Fillmore took office at President Taylor's death.

Abigail Powers Fillmore was the first presidential wife to have a career after marriage. A teacher, she had taught Millard before their wedding in 1826.

DID YOU KNOW . . . ?

- His nickname, the "American Louis-Philippe," came from Fillmore's reputation for a luxurious White House lifestyle that compared with the extravagancies of the recent king of France.
- Fillmore had been indentured to a cloth maker as a young man.
- He installed the White House's first kitchen stove and library.
- Fillmore became chancellor of the University of Buffalo.
- In the TV show *The Brady Bunch*, some of the kids went to Fillmore Junior High.

THE FILLMORE FAMILY

Father Nathaniel Fillmore (1771–1863)

Occupation Farmer

Mother Phoebe Millard Fillmore (1780–1831)

First Wife Abigail Powers Fillmore (1798–1853)

Marriage February 5, 1826

Occupation Teacher

Children Millard Powers (1828–1889); Mary Abigail (1832–54)

Second Wife Caroline Carmichael McIntosh (1813–1881)

Marriage February 10, 1858

Millard and Abigail's daughter, Mary Abigail, known as "Abby," acted as White House hostess when her mother became ill.

Timeline of the Fillmore Presidency

US Events | **World Events**

1850 (US) Congress passes the Compromise of 1850, including the Fugitive Slave Act

1851 (World) First Australian gold rush

1851 (US) The *New York Times* newspaper is founded

1851 (World) The Great Exhibition of London attracts more than six million visitors

1851 (US) Harriet Beecher Stowe publishes *Uncle Tom's Cabin*

1851 (World) Volcano Mount Pelée in Martinique erupts, killing 30 people

1851 (US) Herman Melville publishes *Moby Dick*

1852 (World) First publication of *Roget's Thesaurus*

1852 (World) Founding of the Société Aerostatique, the world's first aeronautical society

1852 (US) Elisha Otis debuts his safety passenger elevator

1853 (World) George Cayley of England develops a working piloted glider

Franklin Pierce

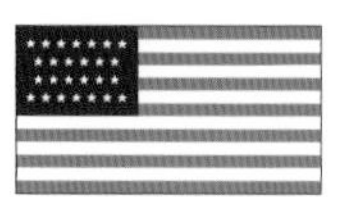

"Handsome Frank"

1853–1857

14th President

Franklin Pierce, a man of great social skill and charm, began his presidency as a dark horse and ended his single term under a dark cloud—one of disappointment and failed policies.

Pierce was born in a log cabin, to a farmer father who would twice become governor of New Hampshire. After attending Bowdoin College in Maine, Pierce studied law in Massachusetts. At the age of 27 he was elected to the House. He later took a seat in the Senate, where he served from 1837 to 1842.

In 1847, during the Mexican-American War, Pierce rose to the rank of brigadier general and fought with Winfield Scott's army.

A Tragic Beginning

During the Democratic Convention of 1852, Pierce was not given much consideration as a nominee. His reluctance to take sides on the slavery issue eventually made him the candidate of choice—because he wouldn't offend anyone.

Sadly, just after Pierce won the election, he and his wife witnessed the death of their 11-year-old son, Benny, in a train derailment. Afterward Jane Pierce suffered serious bouts of melancholy.

The Missouri Compromise Revoked

President Pierce was criticized for filling his cabinet with men of widely differing views, yet it was the only cabinet, as of 2008, that remained intact for a full four years.

"With the Union my best and dearest earthly hopes are entwined."

The Kansas-Nebraska Act shattered the early tranquility of Pierce's term. The act, promoted by Senator Stephen A. Douglas, revoked the Missouri Compromise that had forbidden slavery in the states west and north of Missouri. Douglas virtually threatened Pierce into passing the bill, which led to great unrest in the Midwest states and territories, as pro- and anti-slavery forces battled to gain ground.

When "border ruffians" voted in a pro-slavery government in Kansas, Pierce recognized it, even after a congressional committee declared it illegal. Northern abolitionists, who formed the Republican Party partly in response to the growing strength of the Southern Democrats who clearly had the president in their grip, now hated Pierce.

The Democrats did not renominate Pierce, making him the only elected president ever to be passed over by his party in this way.

Pierce and his wife retired to private life, and he began drinking heavily. Letters he wrote, referring to "the madness of northern abolitionism," destroyed his reputation. During the Civil War he supported the Confederacy, which was headed by his former secretary of war Jefferson Davis.

BIOGRAPHICAL FACTS

Birth November 23, 1804, Hillsboro, New Hampshire

Religion Episcopalian

Education Bowdoin College (graduated 1824)

Occupation Lawyer

Other Offices Member of New Hampshire legislature; member of US House of Representatives; US senator

Military Service Brigadier general in Mexican-American War

Political Party Democratic

Vice President William R. King

Age at Inauguration 48

Death October 8, 1869, Concord, New Hampshire

Brigadier General Pierce, around 1847.

Pierce's inauguration in the Capitol Rotunda. His vice president, William R. King, died just over a month after the inauguration, leaving Pierce with no vice president for the rest of his term.

> "I hope he won't be elected for I should not like to be at Washington and I know you would not either."
>
> —Benny Pierce, in a letter to Jane

DID YOU KNOW...?

- Pierce was sworn in as president using a law book instead of a Bible.
- A popular Democratic campaign slogan was "We Polked you in 1844; we shall Pierce you in 1852."

THE PIERCE FAMILY

Father Benjamin Pierce (1757–1839)

Occupation Farmer; soldier; governor of New Hampshire

Mother Anna Kendrick Pierce (1768–1838)

Wife Jane Means Appleton Pierce

Marriage November 19, 1834

Birth March 12, 1806, Hampton, New Hampshire

Death December 2, 1863, Andover, Massachusetts

Children Franklin (1836); Frank Robert (1839–1843); Benjamin "Benny" (1841–1853)

The untimely deaths of her sons were too much for the fragile Jane Pierce, who suffered from depression.

Timeline of the Pierce Presidency

US Events | **World Events**

1853 Chef George Crum first serves potato chips in Saratoga Springs, New York

1853 Gadsden Purchase of Arizona Territory from Mexico

1854 Commodore Matthew Perry negotiates treaty with Japan

1854 Kansas-Nebraska Act revokes Missouri Compromise

1854 Republican Party forms in part to abolish slavery

1855 German chemist Robert Bunsen invents Bunsen burner

1855 Henry David Thoreau publishes *Walden*

1855 YWCA founded in Britain

1856 British inventor Alexander Parkes creates celluloid, first human-made plastic

1856 Great Train Wreck near Philadelphia, worst train disaster to date

1856 First discovery of Neanderthal remains near Cologne, Germany

1856 Invention of the first synthetic dye

James Buchanan

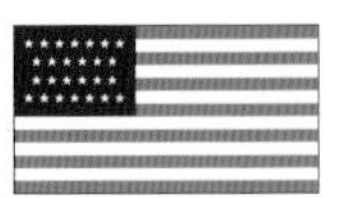

"Old Buck"

1857–1861

Though he had a sharp legal mind and a good eye for details, James Buchanan's flaw as a president was his inability to grasp how badly divided the politics of the country had grown.

Buchanan was born in a log cabin in a frontier settlement in Pennsylvania, where his father ran the trading post. After studying law at Dickinson College, he served five terms in Congress. He was also minister to Russia, spent a decade in the Senate, was secretary of state for James K. Polk, and then minister to Great Britain for Franklin Pierce.

His diplomatic chores had kept him out of heated political disputes at home, and so he appeared to be a neutral candidate for president when the Democrats nominated him in 1856. To maintain this neutrality, Buchanan intended to balance his cabinet between Northern and Southern interests.

Buchanan truly believed that the Constitution would prevent the country from splitting apart. He didn't understand that Northern politicians would reject any interpretation of the Constitution that favored Southern interests, and vice versa.

The Government Stalemate

Shortly before Buchanan took office, two justices hinted to the president-elect that the Supreme Court would limit slavery in new territories. At his inauguration Buchanan shrugged off the looming territorial issue as "happily, a matter of but little practical importance."

When the Supreme Court issued the *Dred Scott* decision just days later—asserting that they had no authority to restrict an individual's right to own property, meaning slaves, in the US territories—Buchanan felt betrayed, and he quickly lost the support of the North. He inflamed the anti-slavery Republicans even further by recommending the admission of Kansas as a slave state. In spite of his urging, Kansas remained a territory.

Even though the Republicans controlled Congress after 1858, Southern congressmen voted down every major bill, or Buchanan vetoed them. The government ground to a standstill.

"Whatever the result may be, I shall carry to my grave the consciousness that I at least meant well for my country."

With the nomination of Abraham Lincoln for president, rumblings of Southern secession grew steadily louder. Buchanan attempted to reach a compromise, but the South refused to negotiate. In January 1861 Buchanan sent reinforcements on a civilian ship, the *Star of the West*, to aid US Fort Sumter in South Carolina, which was under attack by secessionist forces. When battery guns in Charleston harbor fired on the troop ship, they were the first shots of the Civil War.

Leaving newly elected President Lincoln to cope with the Confederacy, Buchanan retired to his home in Pennsylvania, where he died seven years later.

BIOGRAPHICAL FACTS

Birth April 23, 1791, Cove Gap, Pennsylvania

Religion Presbyterian

Education Dickinson College (graduated 1809)

Occupation Lawyer; diplomat

Other Offices Member of Pennsylvania House of Representatives; member of US House of Representatives; minister to Russia; US senator; secretary of state; minister to England

Military Service Light dragoon in Baltimore militia

Political Party Democratic

Vice President John C. Breckinridge

Age at Inauguration 65

Death June 1, 1868, Lancaster, Pennsylvania

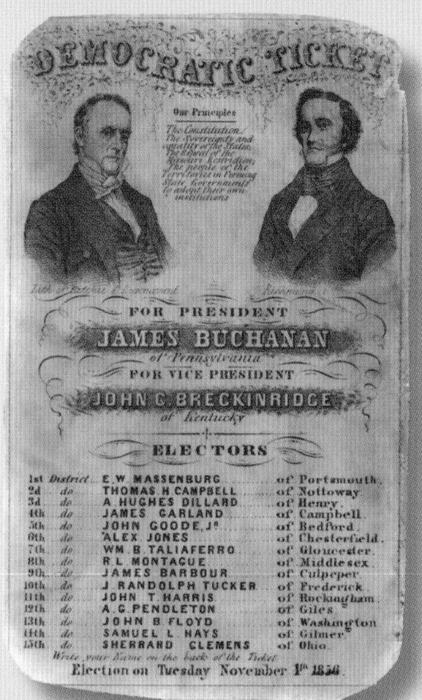

The 1856 Democratic ticket.

Buchanan's 1857 inauguration ball took place in an immense building erected for the purpose in Judiciary Square. After the gloomy Pierce administration, Washington society welcomed the chance to celebrate.

> "I like the noise of democracy."
>
> —James Buchanan

THE BUCHANAN FAMILY

Father James Buchanan Sr. (1761–1821)

Occupation Storekeeper

Mother Elizabeth Speer Buchanan (1767–1833)

Acting as hostess for her bachelor uncle, Harriet Lane filled the White House with gaiety.

DID YOU KNOW...?

- James Buchanan was the only president who never married.
- Buchanan is the only president to hail from Pennsylvania.
- The Buchanan family claimed direct descent from King James I of Scotland.
- James Buchanan was the first president to send a transatlantic telegram.
- A birth defect in his eye caused him to tilt his head forward. This posture made people believe that Buchanan was paying complete attention to them.

Timeline of the Buchanan Presidency

US Events / **World Events**

1858 (US) Philadelphia tinsmith John L. Mason patents screw-on lids for fruit jars, called Mason jars

1858 (World) First publication of *Gray's Anatomy* in Great Britain

1859 (US) Edwin L. Drake perfects new method of drilling for oil

1858 (US) President Buchanan inaugurates transatlantic telegraph with message to Queen Victoria

1859 (World) Jules Leotard, of the Cirque Napoleon, pioneers the circus trapeze

1859 (US) Charles Blondin crosses Niagara Falls on a tightrope

1859 (World) Charles Darwin publishes *Origin of Species*

1859 (World) Rabbits are introduced into Australia

1860 (US) Milton Bradley publishes its first game, called the Checkered Game of Life

1860 (World) First World Heavyweight Boxing Championship is fought

1860 (US) Oliver Winchester patents the repeating rifle

1861 (World) Unification of Italy

Abraham Lincoln

"Honest Abe"

1861–1865

When Abraham Lincoln took office, the nation was at war with itself. Lincoln not only led the United States through one of its darkest eras, he did it with dignity, compassion, wisdom, and even occasional humor.

Lincoln's early life was full of hardship. Born to a poor family on the Kentucky frontier, he was determined to get an education. He worked tirelessly—splitting fence rails and running a store—and studied hard, eventually becoming a country lawyer. After serving as a captain in the Black Hawk War, he spent eight years as a Whig in the Illinois legislature, followed by years of traveling around the state to attend the circuit courts.

After Lincoln served two years as a member of the House, the Republicans chose him to run for the Senate against Democrat Stephen Douglas. The men engaged in seven famous debates, during which Lincoln condemned the immorality of slavery. Even though he lost the election, he'd become a national figure, and the Republicans nominated him for president in 1860. Despite his platform of putting an end to slavery and preserving the Union, the Republicans considered him a moderate who could carry the critical Western states. He won the election with only 40 percent of the popular vote.

Civil War Erupts

Before Lincoln even took the oath of office, seven Southern states seceded from the Union. Lincoln believed secession was illegal, but he was determined to hold off hostilities. Yet when Union-held Fort Sumter fell to the Confederacy in April, he rallied the Northern states to take up arms. In a bold strategic move, he ordered the Union army to gain control of the slave states bordering the Confederacy. He still suffered criticism from all sides: anti-war Copperheads thought he should have compromised on slavery, while the Radical Republicans complained that he should have moved more quickly to free the slaves.

"You have no oath registered in Heaven to destroy the government, while I shall have the most solemn one to preserve, protect and defend it."

After appointing a series of generals to lead the Army of the Potomac, Lincoln found the right person in Ulysses S. Grant. General Robert E. Lee surrendered to Grant in 1865, and Lincoln prepared for rebuilding the South, intending to be flexible and lenient. But before he could put his plans into action, a gunman assassinated him. Much of the nation was shocked and deeply saddened.

Like Washington, Lincoln left a legacy of calm strength under pressure. These two presidents shared the belief that the good of the entire country was more important than the needs of individual states.

BIOGRAPHICAL FACTS

Birth February 12, 1809, Hardin County, Kentucky

Religion No formal religion

Education No formal education

Occupation Lawyer

Other Offices Member of Illinois legislature; member of US House of Representatives

Military Service Captain, Fourth Regiment of Mounted Volunteers, 1832

Political Party Whig; Republican

Vice President Hannibal Hamlin; Andrew Johnson

Age at Inauguration 52

Death April 15, 1865, Washington, DC

LINCOLN'S APPEARANCE

Tall and very lean, Lincoln remained strong and robust his whole life. He was not handsome, but his presence was powerful and arresting. As a writer for the *London Times* reported, "It would not be possible for the most indifferent observer to pass him in the street without notice." Originally clean-shaven, Lincoln, according to reports, grew his beard on the recommendation of an 11-year-old girl who said that whiskers would "look a great deal better, for your face is so thin."

Abraham Lincoln shortly before the 1860 election had yet to grow in his now famous whiskers.

Mary Todd Lincoln, known for her extravagant taste, wears the height of 1860s fashion: a hoop-skirted dress richly decorated with flowers and lace.

> "A capacity, and taste, for reading, gives access to whatever has already been discovered by others. It is the key, or one of the keys, to the already solved problems. And not only so. It gives a relish, and facility, for successfully pursuing the yet unsolved ones."
>
> —Abraham Lincoln

THE LINCOLN FAMILY

Father Thomas Lincoln (1778–1851)

Occupation Farmer; carpenter

Mother Nancy Hanks Lincoln (1784–1818)

Stepmother Sarah Bush Johnston Lincoln (1788–1869)

Wife Mary Todd Lincoln

Marriage November 4, 1842

Birth December 13, 1818, Lexington, Kentucky

Death July 16, 1882, Springfield, Illinois

Children Robert Todd (1843–1926); Edward Baker (1846–1850); William Wallace (1850–1862); Thomas "Tad" (1853–1871)

The Lincolns with sons Willie, at left; Tad, at right; and Robert, standing.

During the 1860 campaign, the Republicans dubbed Lincoln the "Rail Splitter," in honor of the time Lincoln spent doing that job. The name served to remind voters that even a common farm boy could work his way to the top through his own efforts.

LINCOLN'S GENERALS

It was critical for Lincoln to appoint his best generals to oppose the Confederate army's formidable commander, Robert E. Lee. When General George B. McClellan spent months planning his campaign, Lincoln, who wanted a speedy end to the war, replaced him with John Pope, who lost the Second Battle of Bull Run. McClellan returned to win the Battle of Antietam but was relieved by General Ambrose Burnside. After Burnside's defeat at Fredericksburg, Lincoln gave Joseph Hooker the command of the Army of the Potomac. Hooker lost at Chancellorsville, so Lincoln replaced him with George Meade, who won at Gettysburg but let Lee's army slip away.

The president finally turned to a skilled tactician, Ulysses S. Grant, who had been successful in Tennessee. "I cannot spare this man," Lincoln told Grant's critics. "He fights." With the assistance of generals Philip Sheridan and William Tecumseh Sherman, General Grant began to wage total war, not only defeating the Confederate armies but also laying waste to farmland, cities, and towns, weakening the South's ability to continue the fight.

President Lincoln and General George McClellan in the general's tent before the Battle of Antietam in fall 1862. Two years later McClellan challenged Lincoln in the race for the presidency.

FAMOUS WORDS

"Four score and seven years ago our fathers brought forth on this continent a new nation, conceived in Liberty and dedicated to the proposition that all men are created equal."

So begins the famous Gettysburg Address, a short speech delivered by Lincoln while he dedicated the Soldiers' National Cemetery at the site of the Battle of Gettysburg.

The crowd's reaction to the speech, however, was so mild that Lincoln commented that, like a bad plow, it wouldn't "scour." The *Chicago Times* referred to it as "silly, flat and dishwatery utterances." Yet over time it became a one of the most quoted speeches in American history, its final phrases stirring the hearts of all who read it: "that we here highly resolve that these dead shall not have died in vain—that this nation, under God, shall have a new birth of freedom—and that government of the people, by the people, for the people, shall not perish from the earth."

16th President

"His ambition was a little engine that knew no rest."

—William Herndon, Lincoln's law partner

THE LINCOLN MEMORIAL

A statue of the slain president is a feature of the memorial.

Although the soaring Washington Monument dominates the capital's skyline, the country's soul dwells inside the Lincoln Memorial. Many people have gone there to reflect at the feet of the towering statue, created by sculptor Daniel Chester French. Lincoln is seated in repose, his deep-set eyes gazing out toward the Capitol through the columns that line the façade. The words of the Gettysburg Address and his Second Inaugural Address are inscribed on the chamber's sides. In 1963 civil rights activist Dr. Martin Luther King delivered his "I have a dream" speech from the front of the memorial.

FREEING THE SLAVES

A banner celebrating the Emancipation Proclamation.

First announced by President Lincoln on September 22, 1862, the Emancipation Proclamation freed the slaves in the Confederate states. Its aim was to wear down the Confederacy by weakening its economy from within. The proclamation did not free slaves in the border states that had remained with the Union. This came later with the 13th Amendment. Lincoln made it clear that the North was fighting to reunite the country, not to free slaves.

> "Whenever I hear any one arguing for slavery I feel a strong impulse to see it tried on him personally."
>
> —Abraham Lincoln

Tad (shown below with his father) and Willie (above), the youngest Lincoln children, had the run of the White House. The public found the mischievous boys engaging and showered them with gifts, including dogs, rabbits, goats, and ponies.

LINCOLN AT HOME

The president enjoyed quiet evenings at the White House with his wife and three sons gathered around him.

The Lincolns suffered greatly at the loss of their son Willie to typhoid during Abraham's first term. Mary was too overcome with grief to attend the funeral or even get out of bed, while Abraham shut himself inside his room to weep.

The Lincoln marriage was stormy at times. A vivacious, social woman, Mary suffered from frequent emotional distress and was said to be a compulsive shopper. She was also intelligent and well-read, and although she hated that politics took Abraham away from her, she was his staunch supporter.

After the shooting of her husband and then the loss of her son Tad just six years later, Mary plunged into depression. Only one of her children outlived her: Robert Todd Lincoln served as ambassador to Great Britain under Benjamin Harrison and secretary of war to James A. Garfield.

Timeline of the Lincoln Presidency

US Events / **World Events**

1861 (US) John Ericsson launches ironclad ship, USS *Monitor*

1861 (World) Formal emancipation of the serfs in imperial Russia

1862 (US) Julia Ward Howe's "Battle Hymn of the Republic" is published and becomes Union anthem

1862 (World) French scientists Louis Pasteur and Claude Bernard perfect pasteurization process

1863 (US) The Emancipation Proclamation frees slaves in Confederate states

1863 (World) London's Underground railway system opens its first train line

1864 (US) Coinage Act places "In God We Trust" on US coins

1864 (World) The International Red Cross is founded

1865 (US) Lee surrenders at Appomattox; Lincoln assassinated by John Wilkes Booth

1865 (World) Russian novelist Leo Tolstoy publishes *War and Peace*

Assassinations

Assassinating, or killing, a political leader is a practice that goes back to ancient times. A political or religious opponent, a military rival, or even a family member who desired to take power could strike down a leader. Sometimes commoners, poor men angry over harsh conditions, or anarchists, who do not believe in governments at all, kill leaders. Even in the United States, with its guaranteed freedom of speech and its opportunities to vote unpopular leaders out of office, dissatisfied men and women have been driven to strike out at the president.

Abraham Lincoln

Date April 14, 1865 **Assassin** John Wilkes Booth

John Wilkes Booth shot Lincoln while the president watched a play.

The end of the Civil War left many people with lasting resentment against Lincoln. On the evening of April 14, 1865, the president and his wife were seated in a box at Ford's Theater watching the play *Our American Cousin*. Actor John Wilkes Booth, head of a pro-South conspiracy, entered the box and shot Lincoln from behind. Before he fled, Booth leapt from the box to the stage shouting, *"Sic semper tyrannus,"* or "Thus always to tyrants." He broke his leg in the fall. Lincoln died the next day at a boardinghouse across from the theater. His body lay in state in 14 cities on its way to Springfield, Illinois, where it was interred. Booth was shot while hiding in a barn. He died from his wounds, and his fellow conspirators were executed.

James A. Garfield

Date July 2, 1881 **Assassin** Charles J. Guiteau

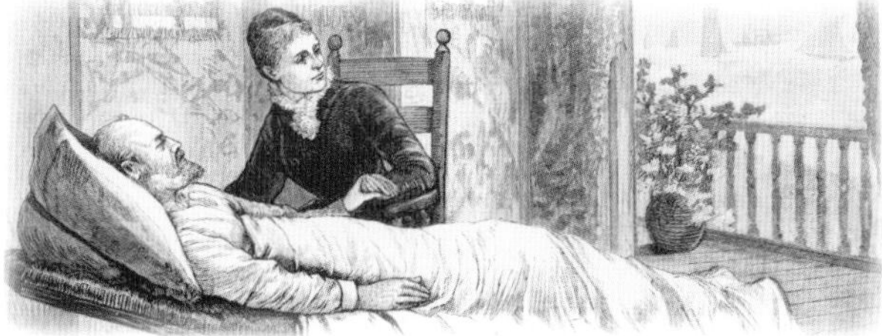

Lucretia Garfield nurses her gravely wounded husband.

Inside a Washington train station, Charles J. Guiteau shot Garfield twice in the back. Secretary of War Robert Todd Lincoln witnessed the attack. Surgeons removed one bullet, but the other was lodged near Garfield's spine. White House physicians probed the wound with bare fingers and unsterilized instruments, trying to remove it. Garfield was transported to a seashore cottage in Elberton, New Jersey, where he died of blood poisoning on September 6. Guiteau, a delusional man with political ambitions, was tried and executed.

William McKinley

Date September 6, 1901 **Assassin** Leon Czolgosz

President McKinley slumps after being hit by Leon Czolgosz's bullets.

Leon Czolgosz twice shot McKinley while the president greeted a reception line at the Pan American Exposition in Buffalo, New York. A self-proclaimed anarchist, Czolgosz had hidden the gun inside a sling supporting his bandaged arm. A button on McKinley's coat deflected one of the bullets, but the other bullet entered the president's stomach, nicking his kidney.

Doctors operated twice, but on September 14 McKinley died from gangrene. His body was returned to Washington, where it lay in state in the East Room of the White House. Czolgosz was tried and executed.

John F. Kennedy

Date November 22, 1963 **Assassin** Lee Harvey Oswald

Just arrived in Dallas, Texas, the president and first lady greet well-wishers. Just a short time later, the Kennedys would begin the fateful motorcade ride.

On November 22, 1963, while he rode in a Dallas motorcade beside the first lady, a bullet pierced Kennedy in the head. Texas governor John Connolly, in the front seat of the car, was also shot. Doctors in Parkland Hospital were unable to revive the president, and an hour later they pronounced him dead. The nation reeled as news of this unexpected tragedy spread. JFK's body lay in state in the Capitol Rotunda until November 25. His funeral procession included Black Jack, a riderless horse with boots reversed in its saddle's stirrups to symbolize the death of the rider. JFK was buried in Arlington National Cemetery in Virginia, where an eternal flame burns in his memory. Dallas nightclub owner Jack Ruby shot and killed suspected assassin Lee Harvey Oswald on November 24, while Oswald was in police custody. The elimination of Oswald before he could "talk" fueled conspiracy theories that he had not acted alone.

"Quiet! I've been shot."

—Theodore Roosevelt, attempting to quiet a panicked crowd

Assassination Attempts

Andrew Jackson

Date January 30, 1835
Attacker Richard Lawrence

Richard Lawrence's two pistols misfired when he attacked the president, who was crossing the Capitol Rotunda. Jackson responded by thrashing the man with his cane. Lawrence, who claimed to be King Richard III of England, was later declared insane.

Richard Lawrence, perpetrator of the first assassination attempt of a US president, takes aim at President Jackson in the Capitol Rotunda.

Theodore Roosevelt

Date October 14, 1912
Attacker John Schrank

Shot in the chest while campaigning in Milwaukee, the rugged Roosevelt continued with his address. His eyeglass case and a sheaf of papers in his pocket reduced the bullet's impact, saving his life. Schrank was declared insane.

Franklin D. Roosevelt

Date February 15, 1933
Attacker Guiseppe Zangara

While Roosevelt was delivering a speech in Miami, Florida, Zangara fired five shots at the president-elect, wounding four people and killing Mayor Anton Cermak of Chicago.

Harry Truman

Date November 1, 1950
Attacker Oscar Collazo, Griseleo Torresola

The two Puerto Rican nationalists attempted to shoot their way into Blair House in Washington. Guards wounded Collazo and killed Torresola.

Gerald R. Ford

Date September 5, 1975
Attacker Lynette Fromme

Fromme aimed a gun at Ford's head but did not fire.

Date September 22, 1975
Attacker Sara Jane Moore

Moore fired at the president but missed. A bystander wrestled her to the ground.

Ronald Reagan

Date March 30, 1981
Attacker John Hinckley Jr.

As Reagan left a Washington hotel, John Hinckley shot the president in the left lung. Hinckley was trying to impress actress Jodie Foster by mimicking a scene from the film *Taxi Driver*.

George W. Bush

Date May 10, 2005
Attacker Vladimir Arutinian

Bush was giving a speech in the country of Georgia when Arutinian threw a hand grenade at him. It failed to detonate.

Andrew Johnson

"The Tennessee Tailor"

1865–1869

Andrew Johnson was the first vice president to take office after the assassination of a chief executive. His greatest challenge was reconciling the economically distressed Southern states with angry Northern states mourning their fallen leader.

Johnson grew up in poverty in North Carolina and, like Lincoln, worked hard to achieve an education. As a young man he opened a tailor shop in Tennessee and then entered politics, becoming a noted stump orator who spoke out against the plantation system. Politically, he fashioned himself after Andrew Jackson. After serving as governor of Tennessee and US congressman, he was elected to the Senate. He chose to remain in office even after the Southern states seceded, making him a hero to Union sympathizers. In 1862 Lincoln appointed him military governor of Tennessee, where Johnson began a reconstruction effort that would become his guide at the end of the Civil War.

Although Johnson was a Southern Democrat, Republican Lincoln chose him to be his running mate in 1864. Five months after their victory, Lincoln was assassinated, and Johnson was now faced with reuniting the country. Johnson began Reconstruction while Congress was not in session, offering amnesty to any Southerners who swore an oath of allegiance. He made little attempt to deal with the problems of the newly freed slaves.

Congress Battles Johnson

When Congress returned to session, the powerful Radical Republicans overturned Johnson's lenient policies. They established military rule in the South, refused congressional seats to any former Confederate politicians, and passed the Civil Rights Act of 1866, which offered US citizenship to blacks. To further protect black Americans, Congress submitted the 14th Amendment, which specified that no state should "deprive any person of life, liberty, or property, without due process of law." Every former Confederate state except Tennessee rejected it.

"Honest conviction is my courage; the Constitution is my guide."

Congress had also imposed a set of restrictions on Johnson to limit his power. When he dismissed Secretary of War Edwin M. Stanton in 1867, the Republicans claimed that he had violated the Tenure of Office Act, which restricted a president's right to replace his cabinet members at will. The Senate brought 11 articles of impeachment, or formal charges, against him. Thirty-five senators voted "guilty" and 19 "not guilty," one vote short of the total votes to impeach the president.

After his term ended, Johnson returned briefly to the Senate. He died in Tennessee in 1875, a stubborn but honorable man who had been placed in a difficult position.

BIOGRAPHICAL FACTS

Birth December 29, 1808, Raleigh, North Carolina

Religion No formal religion

Education No formal education

Occupation Tailor

Other Offices Member of Tennessee State Legislature; member of US House of Representatives; governor of Tennessee; US senator; military governor of Tennessee; vice president

Political Party Democratic

Vice President None

Age at Inauguration 56

Death July 31, 1875, Carter's Station, Tennessee

Andrew, Lillie, and Sarah Stover, children of Johnson's daughter Mary. The president brought much of his close-knit family with him to live at the White House. The Stover children, along with their cousins Mary Belle and Andrew Patterson, attended school in the basement.

Both female and male spectators crowded into the ladies gallery above the Senate chamber to watch the impeachment hearing of President Andrew Johnson.

DID YOU KNOW...?

- Eliza Johnson holds the record among first ladies for wedding the youngest, at age 16.
- Andrew Johnson never attended school and taught himself to read. His wife helped him learn to write and do arithmetic.
- He and his brother were indentured to a tailor as boys but ran away after two years.
- Johnson, who was suffering from typhoid fever during Lincoln's inauguration, took a shot of brandy before the speeches, leading critics to claim that he was drunk.

THE JOHNSON FAMILY

Eliza McCardle Johnson

Father Jacob Johnson (1778–1812)

Occupation Laborer

Mother Mary McDonough Johnson (1783–1856)

Wife Eliza McCardle Johnson

Birth October 4, 1810, Leesburg, Tennessee

Marriage May 5, 1827

Death January 15, 1876, Greeneville, Tennessee

Children
Martha (1828–1901); Charles (1830–1863); Mary (1832–1883); Robert (1834–1869); Andrew (1852–1879)

Timeline of the Johnson Presidency

US Events | **World Events**

1865 (US) Formation of the Ku Klux Klan

1865 (World) William and Catherine Booth found the Salvation Army in London's East End

1866 (US) Civil Rights Act establishes African Americans as citizens and forbids discrimination

1867 (World) The Marquess of Queensbury rules of boxing are laid down

1867 (World) Dominion of Canada is formed

1867 (US) Alaska purchased from the Russian Empire; the frozen land is called Seward's Folly

1867 (World) Swedish scientist Alfred Nobel patents dynamite

1868 (US) An eight-hour workday is established for federal employees

1868 (World) Badminton invented in England

1868 (US) Tabasco sauce invented in Louisiana

1868 (World) The first-ever traffic lights are installed outside the British Houses of Parliament

1869 (US) The Union Pacific and Central Pacific Railways meet

Presidents of the Gilded Age

Tammany Hall, lavishly decorated for the National Convention on July 4, 1868. Tammany Hall was the center of New York City's government—and its corrupt political machine. During the Gilded Age political "bosses," such as Tammany's William M. Tweed and Richard Croker, controlled elections.

As the Industrial Revolution took hold in the United States in the mid-1800s, the factory system began to replace traditional small industries such as weaving, shoemaking, and tanning leather.

> **"So long as all the increased wealth which modern progress brings goes but to build up great fortunes . . . and make sharper the contrast between the House of Have and the House of Want, progress is not real and cannot be permanent."**
>
> —Henry George, *Progress and Poverty*

Factories typically used dozens of large machines to turn out items quickly—and in great volume. Many young women and men from small towns and farms migrated to the cities to find work, most of them laboring in factories for low wages.

The Haves

Factory owners quickly discovered that in addition to manufactured goods, fabulous fortunes could also be made in coal, steel, shipping, and railroads. These newly wealthy tycoons and their families built elaborate, grand mansions where they entertained on an equally grand, often wasteful scale. These extravagancies inspired the nickname "Gilded Age," from the title of a novel by Mark Twain and Charles Dudley Warner that poked fun at the greed and corruption of the era. Twain and Warner were in turn inspired by the Shakespeare quotation "To gild refined gold, to paint the lily . . . is wasteful and ridiculous excess." The nation now had a distinct upper class, similar to that of England's aristocracy.

The Have Nots

In contrast to the riches of the few, there was also crushing poverty for many families during this time. Immigrants from Europe, forced from their homelands by famine or religious persecution, flooded into the United States, seeking the promise of a brighter future. Often all they found was more poverty. But there was opportunity here for many who applied themselves. For the immigrants who did improve their lives, the promise of America—whose streets were supposedly "paved with gold"—was fulfilled. But for the thousands who lived in crumbling city tenements or on hardscrabble farms, poverty was a way of life.

Charities to help the poor, such as the Salvation Army, sprang up across the nation. Many wealthy women and men became philanthropists, giving large sums of money, called endowments, to these charities as well as to universities, hospitals, museums, libraries, and all branches of the arts.

Stopping the Political Machines

This was also an age when the power of political "machines" increased. The press harshly criticized corrupt politicians, such as Boss Tweed in New York City, but it took the intervention of relentless reformers and socially conscious politicians to return fair dealing to the government.

The more forward-thinking presidents worked to address the problems of the poor and battled the rise of corruption. Chester A. Arthur, once part of the Republican political machine, later reformed the civil service and battled the "spoils system." Grover Cleveland opposed high taxes, corruption, and political patronage.

WHAT DOES THAT MEAN?

Civil Service The group of employees in any government agency, except the military

Customs House A building, often in a port city, that housed the offices for officials who processed the paperwork and collected duties for the import and export of goods into and out of a country

Industrial Revolution A period stretching from the late 18th to the late 19th centuries when major changes in agriculture, manufacturing, and transportation profoundly altered social, economic, and cultural conditions in Britain, Europe, and the United States

Jim Crow Laws State and local laws in the Southern and border states that required racial segregation, or separation between white and black Americans

Political Machine An unofficial, behind-the-scenes organization that controls a political party. It often involves politicians giving out favors in return for votes. The machine could influence lawmaking by swaying voters or legislators.

Political Boss An influential politician who ran the machine and handed out appointments or contracts as rewards for loyalty

Although political machines were still a factor in 20th-century politics—notably in Chicago, Illinois, and Louisiana—the power of the "boss" was waning by the end of the 19th century.

The United States kept out of almost all foreign affairs during this era. With the exception of a brief war with Spain in 1898, the nation avoided any major conflicts, more interested in building up its internal resources than looking outward.

THE SPOILS SYSTEM

The spoils system, or giving out government jobs or appointments to people based on their political loyalties rather than their individual abilities, was once far too common. For example, a local politician would make sure that his whole district voted for a certain candidate because he would receive a comfortable job in the city government if that candidate won. The spoils system usually involved *patronage,* or favoring only those in your own party; *cronyism*, or favoring your friends; and *corruption*, or using bribery, threats, or violence to gain votes.

Ulysses S. Grant

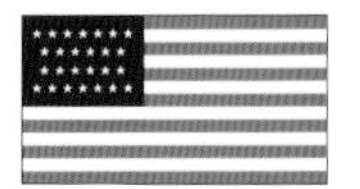

"Hero of Appomattox"

1869–1877

There had been war hero presidents before General Ulysses S. Grant, but none had led the fight to save the Union itself. Yet, although he was a seasoned commander on the battlefield, his lack of political experience caught up with him once he got to Washington.

Grant was born on a farm in Ohio, the son of a tanner. He left home for the military college at West Point in 1839 and after graduation was assigned to St. Louis, where he met his wife, Julia. After two years fighting in the Mexican War, he returned to Galena, Ohio, happy to be home with his family. When the Civil War broke out, the army appointed Grant a colonel in the Illinois infantry, and he quickly rose to the rank of major general.

After Grant achieved a series of victories in the West, Lincoln named him general in chief of the Union forces in March 1864. As a fellow officer said of Grant, "He never lacked in courage, never dodged. He wouldn't as much wink when bullets went whizzing by. He had iron nerves."

The Conquering Hero

By April 1865 the South had run out of resources. After Robert E. Lee surrendered to Grant at Appomattox Court House in Virginia, Grant's eventual election as president now seemed a foregone conclusion. He didn't even bother to campaign, preferring to remain at home in Galena.

As president, Grant often let his personal vanity get in the way of political wisdom. He accepted gifts from favor-seeking admirers and went out on the town with "robber barons" Jay Gould and Jim Fisk. He managed to stop their scheme to corner the gold market but not before it damaged US business.

During his second term Grant met with opposition from liberal Republican reformers, while his supporters in the party became known as the "Old Guard." Though Grant was not a reformer, his administration did see one landmark—the passing of the 15th Amendment, which guaranteed the right to vote to men of all races.

"I know only two tunes: one of them is 'Yankee Doodle,' and the other isn't."

After leaving Washington, Grant and his wife toured the world capitals, where they were received like royalty. When he was diagnosed with throat cancer, Grant, whose brokerage firm had failed, tried to restore the family finances by writing his memoir. He was able to finish the work only days before he died. It became the best-selling book of its era, earning Julia Grant $500,000, and it is still considered the best-written presidential memoir.

BIOGRAPHICAL FACTS

Birth April 27, 1822, Point Pleasant, Ohio

Religion Methodist

Education US Military Academy in West Point, N.Y. (graduated 1843)

Occupation Soldier; railroad president

Military Service General in chief of all US Armies, 1864

Political Party Republican

Vice President Schuyler Colfax; Henry Wilson

Age at Inauguration 46

Death July 23, 1885, Mount McGregor, New York

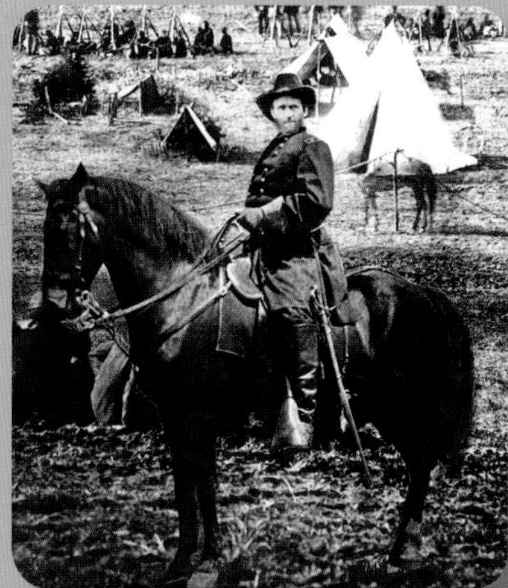

A composite photo shows General Grant on his campaign mount, Cincinnati. Grant was a skilled rider who owned many horses. He allowed only a select few people to ride Cincinnati; one of them was Abraham Lincoln.

A commemorative print from 1870 depicts scenes from 19th-century African American life. It was released to celebrate the passing of the 15th Amendment, which stated that the "right of citizens of the United States to vote shall not be denied or abridged by the United States or by any state on account of race, color, or previous condition of servitude."

DID YOU KNOW . . . ?

- Grant ate a cucumber soaked in vinegar for breakfast each day.
- His real name was Hiram Ulysses Grant. He changed it before entering West Point.
- Grant was the first four-star general in US history.
- The Grants owned a dog named Leo who would catch chickens for the family supper.

THE GRANT FAMILY

Father Jesse Root Grant (1794–1873)

Occupation Tanner

Mother Hannah Simpson Grant (1798–1883)

Wife Julia Boggs Dent

Birth January 26, 1826, near St. Louis, Missouri

Marriage August 22, 1848

Death December 14, 1902, Washington, DC

Children Frederick Dent (1850–1912); Ulysses "Buck" Simpson (1852–1929); Ellen "Nellie" Wrenshall (1855–1922); Jesse Root (1858–1934)

An 1868 print shows the Grant family, from left: Jesse, in front with golf club; Nellie and Fred, standing at back; Buck; Julia; and the president.

Timeline of the Grant Presidency

US Events / **World Events**

1869 (US) Ives W. McGaffey patents the vacuum cleaner

1869 (World) Rickshaw is invented

1870 (World) Mendeleev publishes the periodic table of elements

1871 (US) Barnum's Circus opens at Brooklyn, New York

1871 (US) The Chicago fire rages for three days

1872 (US) First passenger train robbery by the Jesse James gang

1872 (US) Yellowstone National Park, the first national park, is created

1872 (World) English author Lewis Carroll publishes *Through the Looking Glass*

1873 (US) Andrew S. Hallidie introduces the cable car to San Francisco

1874 (US) Joseph F. Glidden patents barbed wire

1875 (World) Electric dental drill is invented

1875 (World) Matthew Webb is first person to swim the English Channel

1876 (US) Baseball's National League is founded

1876 (US) Inventor Alexander Graham Bell patents the telephone

19th President

Rutherford B. Hayes

"Dark-Horse President"

1877–1881

After gaining the presidency in a controversial election, Rutherford B. Hayes brought dignity and moderation to the White House, even to the point of forbidding alcohol.

Early Career

Hayes, who grew up in Ohio, lost his father months before he was born. His mother's brother, Sardis Birchard, stood in as father figure. Hayes graduated from Kenyon College, and after attending Harvard Law School he opened a practice in Cincinnati. There he met and married Lucy Webb.

At the outbreak of the Civil War, Hayes was appointed a major in an Ohio volunteer regiment and served with distinction in the Southern campaign. He was wounded four times in battle before eventually retiring with the rank of brevet major general. During the war Hayes promoted a young private, future president William McKinley, and later contributed to his political success. Hayes was still stationed in Virginia when Ohio Republicans nominated him to a seat in Congress. In spite of refusing to leave his troops to campaign, he won. His two stints in Congress were followed by three terms as governor of Ohio.

A Hotly Contested Election

In 1876 his reputation as a moderate Republican made Hayes the ideal presidential candidate to follow the scandal-ridden Grant. Although Democrat Samuel J. Tilden won the popular vote, the electoral votes were contested in four states.

There were cries of fraud on both sides, and many critics called it the election without "a fair ballot and a fair count." Hayes was finally declared president after he promised Southern Democrats to remove federal troops from the South. This "bargaining" for the presidency led critics to call him "Rutherfraud" B. Hayes.

"He serves his party best who serves his country best."

As president, Hayes worked to end the crippling financial panic of 1873. He also fought Congress to maintain civil rights for black Americans, vetoing four bills until they met with his agenda. Unfortunately, when Hayes ended Reconstruction, he left Southern blacks under the thumb of racist "Redeemer" Democrats. The Redeemers took back most of the rights given to blacks and passed "Jim Crow" laws that imposed segregation. Hayes's darkest moment came after he ordered troops to control rioting workers during the Great Railroad Strike of 1877. Federal troops fired on American citizens, killing more than 70 people.

After he left office, Hayes served on the board of trustees of Ohio State University. When he died from a heart attack in 1893, his last words were, "I know that I'm going where Lucy is."

BIOGRAPHICAL FACTS

Birth October 4, 1822, Delaware, Ohio

Religion Methodist

Education Kenyon College (graduated 1842); Harvard Law School (graduated 1845)

Occupation Lawyer

Other Offices Member of US House of Representatives; governor of Ohio

Military Service Brevet major general, 23rd Ohio Regiment

Political Party Republican

Vice President William A. Wheeler

Age at Inauguration 54

Death January 17, 1893, Fremont, Ohio

Rutherford and Lucy Hayes sit for their wedding portrait, December 30, 1852. The Hayeses later used their private wealth to decorate the White House.

Two children, wearing their Sunday best, pose on the White House lawn, where a crowd has gathered for the 1898 Easter Egg Roll. Lucy Hayes held the first White House Easter Egg Roll in 1878, and the event became an annual tradition.

DID YOU KNOW . . . ?

- Rutherford B. Hayes proposed that presidents serve one six-year term.
- The first lady was known as "Lemonade Lucy" for her refusal to serve alcohol.
- Hayes's prized desk was made of timber from the HMS *Resolute*, a British ship that had been abandoned in the Arctic and later drifted down to the United States.

THE HAYES FAMILY

Father Rutherford Hayes (1787–1822)

Occupation Merchant; farmer

Mother Sophia Birchard Hayes (1792–1866)

Wife Lucy Ware Webb

Birth August 28, 1831, Chillicothe, Ohio

Marriage December 30, 1852

Death June 25, 1889, Fremont, Ohio

Children Birchard Austin (1853–1926); James Webb Cook (1856–1934); Rutherford Platt (1858–1927); Joseph (1861–1863); George Crook (1864–1918); Fanny (1867-1950); Scott Russell (1871–1923); Manning Force (1873–1874)

The Hayes family gathered at Spiegel Grove in Ohio after Rutherford's term had ended. From left: Birchard Hayes, his wife Mary, the president, Scott Hayes, Rutherford Platt Hayes, the first lady, Fanny Hayes, and Webb Hayes.

Timeline of the Hayes Presidency

US Events / **World Events**

1877 (World) First British Open Tennis Championship at Wimbledon

1877 (US) Nez Perce Indians leave Idaho reservation for Canada pursued by US Cavalry

1877 (World) Anna Sewell publishes *Black Beauty*

1878 (US) Cheyenne Indians escape from Indian Territory

1878 (World) Treaty with Samoa makes Pago Pago a coaling station for US Navy ships

1879 (US) Women lawyers argue cases before the Supreme Court for the first time

1879 (World) Britain destroys the Zulu nation in the Zulu War

1879 (US) Thomas Edison develops a practical incandescent light

1879 (World) Mary Baker Eddy charters the Church of Christ, Scientist

1879 (US) The first Woolworth's store opens

1880 (World) Cologne Cathedral in Germany is completed after 634 years; at 515 feet high is the tallest building in the world to date

20th President

James A. Garfield

"The Preacher President" **1881**

James Garfield showed great promise as a president, restoring the strength to the office that had been missing since Lincoln. Yet an assassin's bullet cut his term tragically short. He was the second president struck down while in office.

Garfield was born in rural Ohio and as a young man worked driving canal boat horses to pay for an education. After graduating from Williams College in Massachusetts, he returned to Ohio to teach classical languages at Hiram College. As a measure of his intelligence and ambition, he was named its president within his first year there.

In 1859 Garfield was elected to the Ohio Senate, and in 1861 he favored forcing the Southern states to return to the Union. After he commanded a volunteer brigade in the war—most notably gaining a much-needed victory at Middle Creek, Kentucky—Ohioans elected him to Congress in 1862. He served for 18 years, eventually becoming the leading Republican in the House.

When he supported the presidential nomination of friend John Sherman at the 1880 Republican Convention, Garfield himself ended up as the dark-horse candidate. He won by a narrow margin but without the controversy of the Hayes election.

Battling the Political Machine

Garfield's biggest challenge as president was restoring the authority of the executive office. He met opposition from Senator Roscoe Conkling, a powerful New York Democrat who dispensed political favors and virtually ran the US Customs House in New York City, which controlled the import and export of goods into and out of the country.

When Garfield submitted a list of appointments to the Senate that placed Conkling's rival William Robertson in charge of the Customs House, the New Yorker fought back. Garfield held firm, declaring, "This . . . will settle the question whether the President is registering clerk of the Senate or the Executive of the United States." Conkling resigned in protest, sure his legislature would reelect him, but he was not returned to office. The Senate approved Robertson, and Garfield won a significant victory over the corrupt patronage system.

"Nobody but radicals have ever accomplished anything in a great crisis."

Garfield was also eager to confer with the leaders of the Latin American republics. But on July 2, 1881—long before this groundbreaking summit was to convene—a crazed gunman shot Garfield in a Washington railroad station. Garfield lingered for more than two months as doctors repeatedly attempted to remove the bullet lodged near his spine. After relocating to the New Jersey shore, the ailing president died of blood poisoning.

BIOGRAPHICAL FACTS

Birth November 19, 1831, Orange, Ohio

Religion Disciples of Christ

Education Western Reserve Eclectic Institute; Williams College (graduated 1856)

Occupation Teacher; public official

Other Offices Ohio state senator; member of US House of Representatives; US senator

Military Service Brigadier general, 42nd Ohio Volunteer Infantry

Political Party Republican

Vice President Chester A. Arthur

Age at Inauguration 49

Death September 19, 1881, Elberon, New Jersey

"Be fit for more than the thing you are now doing. . . . If you are not too large for the place you occupy, you are too small for it."

—James A. Garfield

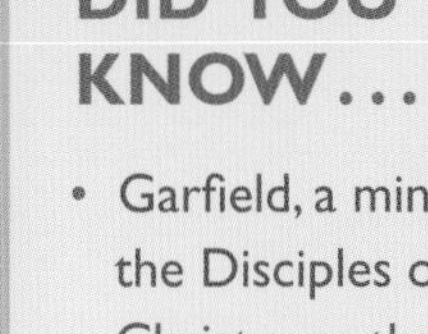

DID YOU KNOW . . . ?

- Garfield, a minister of the Disciples of Christ, was the first and only clergyman president.
- Garfield, New Jersey, was named to honor the president after his funeral train passed through the town.
- Country singer Johnny Cash recorded "Mister Garfield (Has Been Shot Down)."

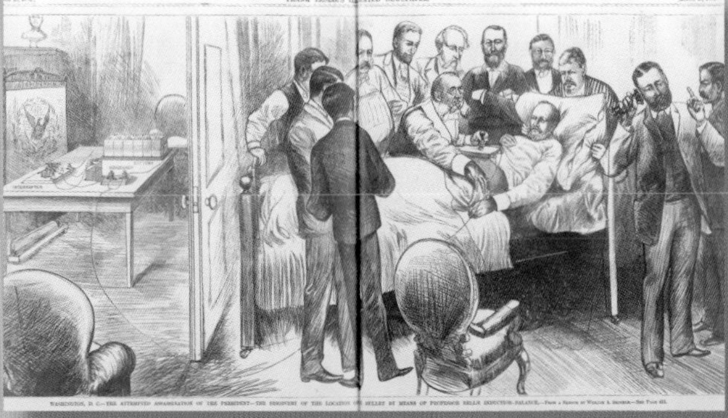

A newspaper illustration depicts inventor Alexander Graham Bell using his induction-balance device to locate the bullet in President Garfield's body.

THE GARFIELD FAMILY

Father Abram Garfield (1799–1833)

Occupation Canal construction supervisor; farmer

Mother Eliza Ballou Garfield (1801–1888)

Wife Lucretia Rudolph Garfield

Birth April 19, 1832, Hiram, Ohio

Marriage November 11, 1858

Death March 14, 1918, South Pasadena, California

Children Eliza (1860–1863); Harry (1863–1942); James (1865–1950); Mary (1867–1947); Irvin (1870–1951); Abram (1872–1958); Edward (1874–1876)

A painting of the Garfield family at home. From left: the first lady, with Abram at her knee in front of the table; Harry; Mary; the president's mother, Eliza; Edward; the president; and Irvin. Behind the table hang portraits of George Washington and Abraham Lincoln.

Timeline of the Garfield Presidency

US Events	World Events
1881 Thomas Edison and Alexander Graham Bell form the Oriental Telephone Company	
	1881 Andrew Watson debuts in Scotland as the first international black footballer
1881 Kansas becomes the first state to prohibit the sale of liquor	
	1881 Tsar Alexander II of Russia is assassinated
1881 Clara Barton establishes the American Red Cross	
	1881 Romania and Serbia win independence from the Ottoman Empire
1881 The United States Tennis Association is founded	
1881 USS *Jeannette* is crushed in Arctic ice pack	
	1881 The Savoy Theatre opens in London, becoming Britain's first public building lit entirely by electricity
1881 Shootout at the OK Corral	

The Vice President

The vice president's duties, as outlined in the Constitution, are to head the Senate and to break tie votes if necessary. The president may also assign the vice president additional responsibilities. Yet even for the most capable politicians, the vice presidency often meant taking a distant back seat to the president when it came to making policy and instituting change. On the other hand, the office elevated each vice president to the national spotlight. In five cases, a vice president was elected president in turn.

The fiery South Carolina politician John C. Calhoun served as vice president under both John Quincy Adams and Andrew Jackson.

An additional nine vice presidents took office at the death or resignation of a chief executive.

It might be said of the position that it became what each vice president chose to make of it. Some were mere figureheads, sent to represent the nation on state occasions, such as ship launchings and funerals of world leaders. Others became part of the president's inner circle, offering advice and helping to shape policy. Still others became gadflies, constantly criticizing weaker presidents and pursuing different agendas.

The Right Running Mate

During a presidential campaign, a party's choice of vice president can play a strategic role in the election. A Northern candidate with a Western running mate can expect to gain a wider range of geographic votes. Or a more liberal candidate might be paired with a moderate or conservative in order to appeal to a greater number of voters. By custom the two candidates do not come from the same state.

Poster from Grover Cleveland's first successful presidential campaign in 1884. It features portraits of both Cleveland and Thomas A. Hendricks labeled with their respective states—New York for the president and Indiana for his running mate.

> "My country has in its wisdom contrived for me the most insignificant office that ever the invention of man contrived or his imagination conceived."
>
> —John Adams

The Vice President Moves Up

As of 2008, 14 vice presidents have gone on to become president. Nine have succeeded to the presidency on the death or resignation of the president: John Tyler, Millard Fillmore, Andrew Johnson, Chester A. Arthur, Theodore Roosevelt, Calvin Coolidge, Harry S. Truman, Lyndon Johnson, and Gerald Ford. Of these, Coolidge, Roosevelt, Truman, and Johnson were then elected to their own terms. Five vice presidents ran for president and were elected: John Adams, Thomas Jefferson, Martin Van Buren, Richard Nixon, and George H. W. Bush.

Notable Vice Presidents

Aaron Burr (1756–1836)

Served under Thomas Jefferson

Burr is best known for killing Alexander Hamilton in a duel, but he was a brilliant man of great ability. Burr disdained public opinion and played at politics as though it were a game of chance. After leaving office he was tried for treason but acquitted.

John C. Calhoun (1782–1850)

Served under John Quincy Adams and Andrew Jackson

This powerful and influential South Carolina politician was a strong supporter of states' rights and of Southern secession.

Garret Hobart (1844–1899)

Served under William McKinley

Hobart was a rarity for his era—a vice president who played an active role in the administration. He was McKinley's close confidant and became known as "assistant to the president."

Hubert Humphrey (1911–1978)

Served under Lyndon Johnson

Nicknamed the "Happy Warrior," Minnesota Democrat Humphrey was voted the most effective senator of the past 50 years by the Associated Press." His refusal to take a strong stand on the Vietnam War may have cost him the White House.

Walter Mondale (b. 1928)

Served under Jimmy Carter

Minnesota Democrat Mondale was the first vice president to have an office inside the White House. He helped shape domestic and foreign policy and became a role model for the strong vice presidents who would follow.

Al Gore Jr. (b. 1948)

Served under Bill Clinton

This Democratic senator from Tennessee narrowly lost a bid for the White House in 2000 but went on to campaign tirelessly against global warming, earning the Nobel Peace Prize in 2007.

Ford, with his wife by his side, takes the oath of office. When Nixon resigned, Ford became the only president never elected as either president or vice president.

A FORD FIRST

Gerald Ford is the only president who ran for neither the presidency nor the vice presidency. Richard Nixon chose him to replace Vice President Spiro Agnew when Agnew stepped down in 1973. When Nixon himself resigned in 1974, Ford became president—without ever being elected to either executive office.

HISTORY OF THE OFFICE

According to the Constitution, the presidency was awarded to the candidate with the majority vote, and the candidate who came in second was named vice president. The Founders contrived this formula before there were separate political parties; however, by the first real election in 1796, there were Federalists and Democratic-Republicans running against each other. When Federalist John Adams won, his opponent, Thomas

George Clinton, the first governor of New York, was also vice president under both Thomas Jefferson and James Madison.

Jefferson, became his vice president. To prevent this conflict from happening again, the 12th Amendment of 1804 specified that the electoral college would vote separately for president and vice president. That way, if a candidate had enough votes to become president, his running mate would likely have enough votes to become vice president.

"Since the start of our nation, the vice presidency has been an awkward office."

—WALTER MONDALE

Chester A. Arthur

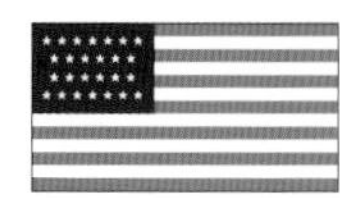

"The Gentleman Boss"

1881–1885

Chester A. Arthur began his political career as part of the Republican machine. When he inherited the presidency under a cloud of suspicion, he put aside party politics and worked hard to vindicate himself.

Arthur was born in Vermont, the son of a Baptist preacher. He graduated from Union College in Schenectady, New York, and worked as a school principal before becoming a lawyer. He opened a practice in New York City where he met his wife, Nell. During the Civil War he served as quartermaster general for the state, earning high praise.

In 1871 at the urging of powerful political boss Roscoe Conkling and the "Stalwart" Republicans, President Grant appointed Arthur to supervise the US Customs House in New York City, which collected import duties. He ran it honestly, but like his fellow Stalwarts he favored the "spoils system"—hiring government employees based on their party support rather than their merits.

In January 1880 Nell died of pneumonia, and a stricken Arthur vowed to never remarry. That same year he agreed to stand as James Garfield's running mate, even though Conkling opposed that move.

Reclaiming His Good Name

Less than three months after Garfield took office, he died. Because his assassin had shouted, "I am a Stalwart . . . Arthur is president now," ugly rumors spread, implicating Arthur in Garfield's death. Determined to prove his worth by rising above party politics and the political machine, Arthur cut himself off from old allies. He then worked for civil service reform, angering the Stalwarts who had profited from the spoils system. The Pendleton Act of 1883 established the Civil Service Commission, which evaluated civil service candidates based on skills, not political ties. Arthur also supported legislation to prevent paupers, criminals, and the mentally ill from entering the country.

"Men may die, but the fabric of free institutions remains unshaken."

It was said that the dapper Arthur "looked like a president," and he enjoyed mingling with high society in Washington, New York, and Newport, Rhode Island. But behind his elegant appearance, he bore a secret sorrow: since his second year in office he had known that he suffered from Bright's disease, a fatal kidney ailment. He chose not to campaign for reelection, and the Republicans did not nominate him for a second term. After leaving office Arthur returned to New York and died a year later from a brain hemorrhage.

Author Mark Twain, rarely complimentary toward politicians, said of him, "It would be hard indeed to better President Arthur's administration."

BIOGRAPHICAL FACTS

Birth October 5, 1830, Fairfield, Vermont
Religion Episcopalian
Education Union College (graduated 1848)
Occupation Lawyer; school principal
Other Offices Quartermaster general of New York State; collector of New York Customs House; vice president
Military Service Brigadier general in New York State Militia
Political Party Republican
Vice President None
Age at Inauguration 50
Death November 18, 1886, New York, New York

President Chester A. Arthur, at center, officially dedicated the magnificent Brooklyn Bridge at its opening in May 1883. Grover Cleveland, then governor of New York, shared the dedication duties.

Ellen "Nell" Herndon Arthur died the year before her husband took office. The grief-stricken Arthur had a memorial stained-glass window made for Nell in a church near his office and asked to have lights kept on so he could see it at night.

DID YOU KNOW . . . ?

- Arthur was a noted fisherman and once caught an 80-pound bass off Rhode Island.
- While redecorating the White House, Arthur had 24 wagon-loads of historic furniture removed and burned.
- The president's sister, Mary Arthur McElroy, served as hostess for her brother.
- Arthur formally dedicated the Washington Monument in February 1885

THE ARTHUR FAMILY

Father William Arthur (1796–1875)
Occupation Baptist minister
Mother Malvina Stone Arthur (1792–1869)
Wife Ellen Lewis Herndon Arthur
Birth August 30, 1837, Fredericksburg, Virginia
Marriage October 25, 1859
Death January 12, 1880, New York, New York
Children William (1860–1863); Chester Alan (1864–1937); Ellen Herndon "Nell" 1871–1915)

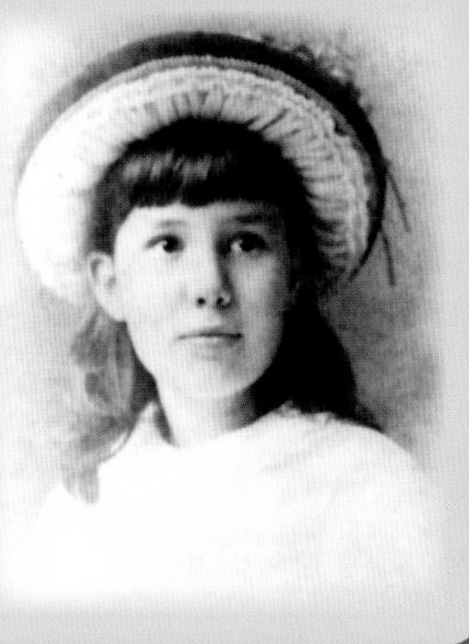

Nell Arthur turned ten a few months after settling into the White House.

Timeline of the Arthur Presidency

US Events | **World Events**

1881 (US) Booker T. Washington founds the Tuskegee Normal and Industrial Institute of Alabama

1883 (World) First journey of the Orient Express from Paris to Constantinople

1883 (US) Louis Waterman invents the capillary-feed fountain pen

1883 (World) Robert Louis Stevenson publishes *Treasure Island*

1883 (World) Mount Krakatoa erupts; it's audible 2,800 miles away.

1884 (US) Cornerstone of the Statue of Liberty base is laid

1884 (World) First edition of the *Oxford English Dictionary* is published

1884 (US) Mark Twain publishes *The Adventures of Huckleberry Finn*

1884 (US) The world's first roller coaster opens at Coney Island

1885 (World) French scientist Louis Pasteur administers a successful rabies vaccine

1885 (US) Dr. Pepper first served

1885 (World) Karl-Friedrich Benz demonstrates the first successful gas-driven motorcar

Grover Cleveland

"Uncle Jumbo" **1885–1889 / 1893–1897**

Reformer Grover Cleveland broke the Republicans' firm hold on the presidency and went on to serve two nonconsecutive terms.

The son of a Presbyterian minister, Cleveland was born in New Jersey and grew up in central New York State. Although not formally educated, he was hired as a law clerk in Buffalo and practiced law for more than two decades. In 1881 Cleveland was elected mayor of Buffalo, partially for his promise to battle a corrupt political machine. His local success led to his election as governor of New York, where he continued to oppose corrupt politicians, even those in his own party, such as powerful Boss Kelly of New York City's Tammany Hall.

In 1884 the Democratic Party chose Cleveland, known for his honesty and idealism, to run for president against James G. Blaine of Maine, who was considered immoral and ambitious. Anti-Blaine Republicans, called "Mugwumps," also supported Cleveland, helping to ensure his election.

As president, Cleveland chose to keep on any Republican appointees who were doing their jobs well and refused to hire anyone based on party loyalty. He also trimmed the overflowing ranks of government workers hired by the spoils system.

The Veto King

Cleveland frequently employed the presidential veto, believing it was his duty to overrule the "bad ideas" of Congress. He also forced the railroads to return 81 million acres of Western land that they had claimed illegally and attempted the first federal regulation of the railroads with the Interstate Commerce Act. His fight to lower high protective tariffs failed.

Cleveland was against expansionism and did not further the plans President Arthur had made to build a canal in Nicaragua. Cleveland called it an "entangling alliance."

While in office Cleveland courted and married Frances Folsom, the college-age daughter of a friend. He was the only president to host his own wedding ceremony in the White House.

"Officeholders are the agents of the people, not their masters."

Cleveland lost the election in 1888 to Benjamin Harrison but ran again in 1892 and won. During his second term he dealt with the financial panic of 1893 and the ensuing national depression by working with Wall Street to keep the nation solvent.

During the Pullman strike of 1894, he sent troops to control strikers, angering the unions. The Democrats were unhappy with his handling of the depression and did not renominate him in 1892.

Cleveland retired with his family to Princeton, New Jersey, where he died in 1908.

BIOGRAPHICAL FACTS

Birth March 18, 1837, Caldwell, New Jersey
Religion Presbyterian
Education No formal education
Occupation Lawyer
Other Offices Sheriff of Erie County; mayor of Buffalo; governor of New York
Political Party Democratic
Vice President Thomas A. Hendricks; Adlai E. Stevenson
Age at Inauguration 47
Death June 24, 1908, Princeton, New Jersey

There have been many White House weddings, but the Cleveland-Folsom wedding is still the only wedding of a sitting president.

Upon her engagement to Grover Cleveland in May 1886, Frances Folsom shot to instant national celebrity.

DID YOU KNOW . . . ?

- Christened Stephen Grover Cleveland, the president never used his first name as an adult.
- Cleveland opposed the women's suffrage movement, which supported a woman's right to vote.
- While campaigning for president Cleveland was accused of fathering a child out of wedlock. This led to the opposition chant of "Ma, Ma, where's my Pa?"

THE CLEVELAND FAMILY

Father Richard Falley Cleveland (1804–1853)
Occupation Minister
Mother Anne Neal Cleveland (1806–1882)
Wife Frances Folsom Cleveland
Birth July 21, 1864, Buffalo, New York

Grover and Frances Cleveland with daughter Esther, the only child of a president to be born in the White House. The American public loved images of her and sister "Baby Ruth."

Marriage June 2, 1886
Death October 29, 1947, Baltimore, Maryland
Children Ruth (1891–1904); Esther (1893–1980); Marion (1895–1977); Richard (1897–1974); Francis Grover (1903–1995)

Timeline of the Cleveland Presidency

US Events | **World Events**

1886 (US) Sears, Roebuck and Co. founded

1886 (US) Coca-Cola goes on sale

1888 (World) The "Jack the Ripper" murders occur in Whitechapel, London

1888 (US) Joseph Assheton Fincher invents the game Tiddlywinks

1888 (US) Eastman's Kodak camera launches photography craze

1888 (US) First issue of *National Geographic Magazine*

1894 (World) London's Tower Bridge completed

1895 (World) British author H. G. Wells publishes *The Time Machine*

1895 (US) First professional football game

1895 (World) William Roentgen discovers X-rays

1896 (US) Thomas Armat's "Vitascope" film projector first used in public

1896 (World) The Klondike gold rush begins in Canada's Yukon Territory

1896 (World) World's first permanent radio station set up

1896 (World) New Zealand women gain voting rights

Benjamin Harrison

"Little Ben"

1889–1893

The grandson of William Henry Harrison, Benjamin Harrison followed his grandfather to the White House—48 years later. As president he was known for high protective tariffs and federal spending as well as for coping with economic woes and Native American issues.

Born at Point Farm, his father's home in Ohio, Harrison attended Miami College in Oxford, Ohio. It was there he met his future wife, Caroline Scott. While working as a law clerk in Indianapolis, Indiana, he became involved in Republican politics and was soon known as a persuasive campaign speaker. During the Civil War he formed a volunteer regiment and fought with distinction in the Atlanta campaign.

After an unsuccessful bid for Indiana governor, state voters elected him to the US Senate in 1881 where he spoke in support of Civil War veterans, homesteaders, and Indians. In 1888 he ran for president as a dark-horse candidate, and, although he received fewer popular votes than Cleveland, the electoral college named him president.

A Troubled Presidency

Congress never warmed up to President Harrison, leaving him with little support for his policies. He continued to make cautious improvements in the civil service—too slowly for the reformers and too quickly for those seeking spoils. Harrison also had difficulty keeping the economy stable, and when the price of silver fell, he barely avoided two national panics. Although the McKinley Tariff Act of 1890 bolstered American manufacturing by raising duties on imported goods and resulted in a government surplus, the surplus had dwindled dangerously by the end of Harrison's term.

Harrison strengthened both the navy and the merchant marine, protecting the country's interests abroad and expanding trade. He did realize Garfield's dream of a Pan-American Conference in 1889, which improved ties between the United States and the Latin American republics.

When Harrison extended the border of Nebraska into the Dakota Territory in 1890, he decreed that any Indian claims to the area had been "extinguished." The government forced many tribes onto reservations where they could no longer sustain their ways of life.

"We Americans have no commission from God to police the world."

Harrison was the first president to request a billion dollars for federal spending. When critics attacked him for his "billion-dollar Congress," Speaker Thomas B. Reed came to his defense, saying, "This is a billion-dollar country."

In 1892 voters reelected Grover Cleveland. Harrison, now widowed, retired to Indianapolis and later married Mary Dimmick, his wife's niece. He died from complications of the flu in 1901.

BIOGRAPHICAL FACTS

Birth August 20, 1833, North Bend, Ohio

Religion Presbyterian

Education Miami University (graduated 1852)

Occupation Lawyer

Other Offices US senator

Military Service Brigadier general, 70th Indiana Volunteer Infantry

Political Party Republican

Vice President Levi P. Morton

Age at Inauguration 55

Death March 13, 1901, Indianapolis, Indiana

> "Great lives never go out; they go on."
>
> —Benjamin Harrison

DID YOU KNOW . . . ?

His Whiskers, the White House goat, stands ready to pull Harrison's grandchildren Mary and "Baby" McKee on the White House lawn while their uncle Major Russell Harrison poses with his daughter, Marthena, and a canine companion.

- Harrison gave his grandchildren a pet goat named His Whiskers who pulled them in a cart. One day His Whiskers took off through the White House gates with President Harrison in pursuit.
- The Harrisons also had two pet opossums named Mr. Reciprocity and Mr. Protection.

First Lady Caroline Harrison introduced the first Christmas tree to the White House.

THE HARRISON FAMILY

Father John Scott Harrison (1804–1878)

Occupation Farmer; politician

Mother Elizabeth Ramsey Irwin Harrison (1810–1850)

First Wife Caroline Lavinia Scott Harrison (1832–1892)

Marriage October 20, 1853

Children Russell Benjamin (1854–1936); Mary Scott (1858–1930)

Second Wife Mary Scott Lord Dimmick Harrison (1858–1948)

Marriage April 6, 1896

Children Elizabeth Harrison (1897–1955)

Four generations of the Scott family. At left is Caroline Scott Harrison, holding her grandson "Baby" McKee. Standing is Mary Scott Harrison McKee. The first lady's father, the Rev. Dr. John Scott, holds Mary Lodge McKee.

Timeline of the Harrison Presidency

US Events | **World Events**

1889 (US) Oklahoma Land Rush begins; 1.9 million acres made available to settlers

1889 (World) Alexandre Gustave Eiffel completes construction of Eiffel Tower in Paris

1890 (US) Whitcomb L. Judson invents the zipper

1890 (US) US Cavalry massacre Sioux Indians at Wounded Knee

1890 (US) Eveready Company produces first dry-cell batteries

1891 (World) British author Arthur Conan Doyle publishes *The Adventures of Sherlock Holmes*

1891 (US) James Naismith invents basketball

1892 (World) Ellis Island, a station for processing immigrants, opens in New York Bay

1892 (World) German engineer Rudolph Diesel patents the internal combustion engine

1893 (US) Lizzie Borden tried and acquitted of murdering her parents

1893 (US) World's Columbian Exhibition, featuring the White City, opens in Chicago

The Cabinet

George Washington held the first recorded meeting of his cabinet in 1791. A cabinet is a group of trusted advisors to whom the president turns for counsel. The cabinet includes the vice president, the attorney general, and the heads, or secretaries, of 14 executive branch departments. The president usually meets with the cabinet once a week to discuss important issues or to resolve problems. Other government officials with areas of expertise, such as the director of the CIA or the US representative to the United Nations, may also sit in on these meetings.

"If I become president, I will have a Cabinet that looks like America."

—Bill Clinton

After the president chooses the cabinet members, the Senate must approve the choices by a simple majority vote. Secretaries cannot hold any elected office while serving, and they normally serve until the president's term is over. It's customary for the old cabinet to resign when a new president takes office, allowing the president to handpick a new group. New departments can be created as needed, such as the Department of Homeland Security, which was formed after the terrorist attacks of September 11, 2001.

The James K. Polk cabinet gathered with the president (third from left) for the first-ever photograph of an American cabinet. Only James Buchanan, secretary of state, is missing. Shot in the State Dining Room, it is also the first photograph taken of the White House interior.

A rare gathering: Ronald Reagan's entire cabinet in 1984.

A CAUTIOUS CABINET

Cabinet members are in the line of succession to the presidency, behind the vice president, the Speaker of the House, and the president *pro tempore* of the Senate. Because of this, it is very rare that the entire cabinet is present in one location. When the cabinet appears in public, at least one member does not attend. This member, called the "designated survivor," is held at a secure location, ready to take over if the president, vice president, member of Congress, and the other cabinet members come to harm.

THE BIG FOUR

Traditionally the president's most important advisors are the secretary of state, the secretary of the treasury, the secretary of defense, and the attorney general. In recent years, the secretary of homeland security has become increasingly powerful.

Condoleezza Rice served as one of George W. Bush's secretaries of state. As the oldest post, the secretary of state is the first cabinet member in the presidential line of succession.

The Members of the President's Cabinet

Here is a list of the 15 executive department secretaries in order of importance, with year of creation and a brief description of each department's responsibilities:

Secretary of State

Year Created 1789

The State Department deals with foreign affairs.

Secretary of the Treasury

Year Created 1789

The Treasury supervises the collection of taxes and the printing of money.

Secretary of Defense

Year Created 1947

The Defense Department oversees the armed forces.

Attorney General

Year Created 1870

The Department of Justice enforces US government laws.

Secretary of the Interior

Year Created 1849

The Department of the Interior protects natural resources and wildlife.

Secretary of Agriculture

Year Created 1862

The Department of Agriculture ensures a healthy food supply and provides support for farmers.

Secretary of Commerce

Year Created 1903

The Commerce Department promotes business and job opportunities. It oversees and grants all copyrights, patents, and trademarks, and oversees matters related to oceans, weather, and technology.

Seal of the Department of Education. Each cabinet department has an official emblem.

Secretary of Labor

Year Created 1913

The Department of Labor oversees the interests of US workers.

Secretary of Health and Human Services

Year Created 1953

Health and Human Services looks after public health and provides services, including conducting medical research, preventing diseases, and assuring the safety of food and drugs. It also provides financial assistance for low-income families.

Secretary of Housing and Urban Development

Year Created 1965

Housing and Urban Development oversees housing needs and focuses on improving and developing communities.

Secretary of Transportation

Year Created 1966

The Transportation Department oversees transportation systems including highways, railroads, ports, and air travel.

Secretary of Energy

Year Created 1977

The Department of Energy is responsible for advancing the nation's energy security and promoting innovation and environmental responsibility.

Secretary of Education

Year Created 1979

The Department of Education establishes guidelines and provides leadership to improve education and helps local communities meet the needs of their students.

Secretary of Veterans Affairs

Year Created 1988

Veterans Affairs operates programs for veterans and their families.

Secretary of Homeland Security

Year Created 2003

The Department of Homeland Security works to prevent terrorist attacks within the United States, reduce vulnerability to terrorism, and minimize the damage from potential attacks and natural disasters.

There are also six non-secretaries who may attend cabinet meetings: the vice president, the White House chief of staff, the administrator of the Environmental Protection Agency, the director of the Office of Management and Budget, the director of the National Drug Control Policy, and the United States trade representative.

William McKinley

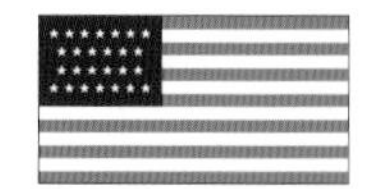

"Idol of Ohio" **1897–1901**

When they chose him as the Republican presidential candidate during an economic depression, his supporters labeled William McKinley as "the advance agent of prosperity." But President McKinley, the popular victor in a war freeing Cuba from Spanish domination, was assassinated at the beginning of his second term.

A lifelong resident of Ohio, McKinley attended Allegheny College for one year before enlisting in the Union army. While he was a private fighting in western Virginia, his commander, future president Rutherford B. Hayes, promoted him for bravery several times. After the war McKinley attended Albany Law School in New York and returned to Ohio to practice law. His introduction to politics was campaigning for his former commander when Hayes was running for governor of Ohio.

Hayes in turn supported McKinley's bid for Congress in 1876, and the young politician served two terms there before becoming governor himself. His claim to fame while in Congress was creating the McKinley Tariff, the highest tariff in US history, which may have lost him his seat in Congress. During his two terms as Ohio governor, he taxed corporations, approved safety legislation for transportation workers, and set restrictions on companies with anti-union policies.

Pamphlets, Posters, and Parades

At the urging of campaign manager Mark Hanna, McKinley set his sights on the presidency in 1896. Hanna raised more than three million dollars to pay for pamphlets, posters, and parades supporting McKinley—ushering in a new era in campaign tactics. Running on a platform of prosperity for all Americans, McKinley easily beat opponent William Jennings Bryan.

"War should never be entered upon until every agency of peace has failed."

McKinley's first term was marked by renewed confidence in the government as industry and agriculture thrived. In 1898 rumors of civil unrest in Cuba spread to the United States, and the navy sent the battleship *Maine* to Havana to protect American interests there. When it blew up in the harbor under mysterious circumstances, outraged Americans demanded war with Spain, and Congress complied. After 113 days the Spanish-American War ended, and the United States gained the Philippines, Guam, and Puerto Rico, as well as temporary control of Cuba.

McKinley again bested Bryan in the 1900 election by focusing on foreign policy. In September 1901, while McKinley attended the Pan-American Exposition in Buffalo, anarchist Leon Czolgosz shot him twice. Surgeons removed one bullet, and the president lingered for eight days before dying of complications from the remaining bullet.

BIOGRAPHICAL FACTS

Birth January 29, 1843, Niles, Ohio

Religion Methodist

Education Allegheny College

Occupation Lawyer

Other Offices Member of US House of Representatives; governor of Ohio

Military Service Brevet major, 23rd Regiment Ohio Volunteers

Political Party Republican

Vice President Garret A. Hobart; Theodore Roosevelt

Age at Inauguration 54

Death September 14, 1901, Buffalo, New York

A campaign poster from the election of 1896 promotes William McKinley and his running mate, Garret A. Hobart.

Ida McKinley. The McKinleys' devotion to each other was clear to all who saw them. Jennie Hobart, wife of Vice President Hobart, noted that their love was "one of those rare and beautiful things that live only in tradition."

DID YOU KNOW . . . ?

- McKinley was the last Civil War veteran elected president.
- An X-ray machine was displayed at the Pan-American Exposition but was not used to locate the bullet in McKinley's back for fear of side effects.
- Mount McKinley in Alaska is named after President McKinley, as are a number of counties, towns, and streets.

Nothing can make me happy again."

—Ida McKinley, after the assassination

THE McKINLEY FAMILY

Father William McKinley Sr. (1807–1892)

Occupation Iron manufacturer

Mother Nancy Campbell Allison McKinley (1809–1897)

Wife Ida Saxton McKinley

Birth June 8, 1847, Canton, Ohio

Occupation Bank cashier

Marriage January 25, 1871

Death May 26, 1907, Canton, Ohio

Children Katherine (1871–1875); Ida (1873)

The graves of Katie and Ida McKinley in Canton, Ohio. The shock of her baby daughters' deaths within two years of each other devastated the first lady.

Timeline of the McKinley Presidency

US Events | **World Events**

1897 (US) Jesse Reno introduces the modern escalator

1897 (US) Hawaii is annexed to the United States

1898 (World) Spanish-American War begins and ends

1898 (US) Joshua Slocum is first person to sail solo around the world

1898 (World) H. G. Wells publishes *The War of the Worlds*

1898 (US) Pepsi Cola is invented

1898–1902 (World) Cuba occupied by United States

1899 (World) Von Zeppelin introduces the rigid dirigible airship

1900 (US) Louis Lassen invents the hamburger in Connecticut

1900 (World) Harry Houdini launches his career as an escape artist

1900 (World) World population is 1.65 billion

1901 (US) Native American Five Civilized Tribes granted US citizenship

1901 (US) King C. Gillette introduces the first disposable razor blade

Presidents of an Emerging Power

A World War I poster for Liberty Bonds depicts the figure of Liberty leading soldiers into battle, carrying an American flag and accompanied by a bald eagle (symbols of the United States). Although the United States began the 20th century isolated from global politics, in its first half the nation entered into two world wars. Victories in these conflicts helped launch the United States into its role of "superpower" during the century's second half.

At the beginning of the 20th century the United States found itself poised on the brink of great changes and even greater challenges. During the first half of the century, presidents would face problems their predecessors never dreamed of: world wars, a catastrophic depression, race riots, and deadly epidemics. Yet they would also see advances in science and technology and in education and human relations that would ensure the nation's status as a world leader.

"The twentieth century looms before us big with the fate of many nations. If we stand idly by . . . the bolder and stronger peoples will pass us by, and will win for themselves the domination of the world."

—Theodore Roosevelt

After 1900 the US population increased dramatically (by 20 percent in the century's first decade alone), swelled by millions of Eastern European, Asian, and Mediterranean immigrants. In this new "melting pot" of ethnic diversity, some Americans viewed these "foreigners" as competitors for jobs and housing, even though their own ancestors had once been immigrants themselves. And immigrants as well as US workers continued to flock to the booming centers of industry: Pittsburgh, Chicago, New York, and Detroit. The urbanization of America had begun: by 1910 only half of the nation remained rural.

Social reformers helped to reduce political corruption, labor unions to improve working conditions, and suffragists to allow women to take their places in the polling booth. Black Americans in the South and elsewhere were still restricted by segregation and other racist practices. Yet as many blacks migrated to northern cities for work, they formed urban communities—with churches and newspapers that gave voice to their demands for equality.

Technology advanced rapidly. In the early 20th century the horse and carriage gave way to the automobile, and humans took to the skies in airplanes. Sailing ships gave way to merchant steamers, battleships, and great ocean liners. In cities nationwide, towering skyscrapers, true marvels of engineering, recast the skyline. Medicine took major steps toward combating epidemic diseases, such as yellow fever and influenza.

The Country Steps Up

Industry continued to thrive. Steel mills, oil refineries, meatpacking plants, and transportation services earned many millions of dollars each year, and in one short decade—from 1900 to 1910—the country's economy nearly doubled.

This rise in industrial strength placed the United States on equal footing with the leading nations of Europe, provoking Theodore Roosevelt to declare that America must step up and take its place as a world power. The chance to do this arose in 1914, when political unrest in Europe and the Far East came to a head. At the urging of Woodrow Wilson, the United States was forced to shed its cocoon of isolationism and take part in a world war. America emerged victorious, its place as a world power now secure.

Yet barely ten years later, the inflated stock market crashed, and the country entered a devastating financial depression. With millions of people out of work, evicted families took to the roads and headed west in a second national migration. Presidents Herbert Hoover and Franklin Roosevelt both attempted to resolve the crisis and reassure struggling citizens that prosperity was around the corner. Ironically, it took a second world war for America to rally, rebuilding its industry and restoring its economy.

And so the relative calm and security of the Gilded Age gave way to a bustling Age of Steel and a United States that was more modern, more powerful—and often more troubled.

WHAT DOES THAT MEAN?

Depression A period of low general economic activity marked especially by rising levels of unemployment

Isolationism A policy of national isolation that includes avoiding alliances and other international political and economic relations

New Deal Programs Franklin Roosevelt initiated between 1933 and 1938 to give relief to the American people and stimulated economic recovery during the Great Depression

Roaring Twenties Name given to the 1920s to emphasize the era's prosperity and focus on all things modern

Suffragist A supporter of women's suffrage, a woman's right to vote

Trust A combination of corporations or companies formed by a legal agreement; trusts tend to unfairly reduce competition and keep prices high

Urbanization The process of an undeveloped rural area (country) evolving into a developed urban area (city)

THE WORLD WARS

Two global conflicts scarred the 20th century. Fought mainly in Europe, World War I, also known as the First World War and the Great War, took place from 1914 to 1918 and resulted in 20 million military and civilian deaths. World War II, or the Second World War, joined what had initially been two separate conflicts: the Second Sino-Japanese War, which started in 1937, and the European conflict that began with the German invasion of Poland in 1939. By 1945 the war had claimed more than 60 million lives, making it the deadliest conflict in human history.

26th President

Theodore Roosevelt

"The Hero of San Juan Hill"

1901–1909

Theodore Roosevelt brought a dynamic energy and a forward-thinking agenda to the White House. He broadened the range of executive power, and his "big stick" foreign policy marked an end to America's isolation from the world stage.

Roosevelt was born in New York City, the son of a wealthy merchant. Because Roosevelt was sickly and asthmatic as a child, his father had him take up boxing to improve his stamina. Roosevelt remained an advocate of strenuous exercise his entire life, and while at Harvard, he rowed crew and boxed—and was known for his good sportsmanship.

He entered Columbia Law School but dropped out in 1881 to join the New York Assembly, where he wrote more bills than any other legislator. When his wife, Alice, died of a kidney ailment shortly after giving birth to a daughter, and his mother died of typhoid—on the same day—he fled to a South Dakota ranch. He stayed two years, living the hardy cowboy life and recovering his spirits. In 1886 he married Edith Kermit Carow, his childhood sweetheart. They settled at Sagamore Hill, the Roosevelt home in Oyster Bay, New York, and Roosevelt returned to politics with renewed vigor. He served as police commissioner of New York and then as assistant secretary of the navy.

At the outbreak of war with Spain, he organized the Rough Riders, a diverse cavalry unit made up of both Westerners and Easterners. Their assault on San Juan Hill in Cuba became part of American mythology, and for his bravery Roosevelt was posthumously awarded the Medal of Honor in 2001.

The Square Dealer

New York voters elected Roosevelt as governor in 1898, and two years later the Republicans chose him as William McKinley's running mate. After McKinley's assassination, a cautious Roosevelt continued the slain president's policies and retained his cabinet. He averted a national crisis by resolving the coal strike in 1902 and issued 44 lawsuits against large corporations, earning himself the nickname "Trustbuster Teddy." After winning the 1904 election he introduced further progressive policies. For example, he approved the Pure Food and Drug Act and the Meat Inspection Act, aimed at safeguarding the public health. He also improved working conditions for women and children.

"The worst of all fears is the fear of living."

In 1906, after negotiating peace between Japan and Russia, Roosevelt received the Nobel Peace Prize. He chose not to run for a second full term in 1908 but ran again in 1912 as the Bull Moose candidate—and lost. After contracting malaria during an ill-fated trip to the Brazilian jungle, he retired to Sagamore Hill. He died there in 1919, just a year after his youngest son, Quentin, had been shot down in World War I.

BIOGRAPHICAL FACTS

Birth October 27, 1858, New York, New York

Religion Dutch Reformed

Education Harvard University (graduated 1880)

Occupation Author; lawyer; public official

Other Offices Member of New York State Assembly; member of Civil Service Commission; assistant secretary of the navy; governor of New York; vice president

Military Service Lieutenant colonel, First US Volunteer Cavalry

Political Party Republican

Vice President Charles Warren Fairbanks

Age at Inauguration 43

Death January 6, 1919, Oyster Bay, New York

Roosevelt was 26 when he dressed up as a Badlands hunter for this photo taken in a New York City studio.

Roosevelt's first wife, Alice Lee. After Alice's sudden death, the grieving Roosevelt left his infant daughter in the care of his sister Anna and headed out to a ranch in South Dakota.

After reading about Roosevelt refusing to shoot a bear cub on a hunting trip, a toy designer came up with the idea of "Teddy's bear." The stuffed animal was an instant hit.

"Character, in the long run, is the decisive factor in the life of an individual and of nations alike."

—Theodore Roosevelt

DID YOU KNOW...?

- When Booker T. Washington was invited to dine with Roosevelt, he became the first African American to make an official visit to the White House.
- Roosevelt approved the first coin with a man's face on it: the Lincoln penny.
- Little Texas was the horse Roosevelt rode up San Juan Hill.
- Roosevelt was blind in one eye, the result of a boxing accident.
- One of his nicknames was "TR," making him the first president to be known by his initials.
- Roosevelt was a great supporter of the Boy Scouts of America and was given the title Chief Scout Citizen.
- Roosevelt was one of the last people to see a live passenger pigeon.

THE ROOSEVELT FAMILY

Father Theodore Roosevelt (1832–1878)

Occupation Glass dealer

Mother Martha Bulloch Roosevelt (1836–1884)

First Wife Alice Hathaway Lee Roosevelt (1861–1884)

Marriage October 27, 1880

Children Alice Lee Roosevelt (1884–1980)

Second Wife Edith Kermit Carow Roosevelt (1861–1948)

Marriage December 2, 1886

Children Theodore Jr. (1887–1944); Kermit (1889–1943); Ethel Carow (1891–1977); Archibald Bulloch (1894–1979); Quentin (1897–1918)

The first family in 1903, from left: Quentin, the president, Theodore Jr., Archie, Alice, Kermit, the first lady, and Ethel. Even though the Roosevelts undertook a major renovation of the mansion, the family thoroughly enjoyed their White House stay.

Alice Lee Roosevelt was the president's daughter by his first wife. The spirited teenager kept a pet snake at the White House that she called "Emily Spinach." When a friend criticized Alice for outrageous behavior, Roosevelt explained, "I can be President of the United States, or I can control Alice. I cannot possibly do both."

ROOSEVELT THE CONSERVATIONIST

Roosevelt was the first president to recognize that the natural resources of the country needed to be protected from development and exploitation. He urged the creation of a national forest service and set aside more land for national parks and nature preserves than all previous presidents combined. By the end of his second term, he had established 42 million acres of national forests and 53 national wildlife refuges. He also protected scientific and archeological sites and created "special interest" areas, such as the Grand Canyon.

Roosevelt and Sierra Club founder John Muir on Glacier Point, Yosemite Valley, California. The president worked with the preservationist to set up the national parks and wildlife refuges that preserved vast acres of wilderness.

Edith Roosevelt with her daughter, Ethel. The first lady was a calming influence in a family of oversize personalities.

> "You must always remember that the president is about six."
>
> —An ambassador, commenting on Roosevelt's boundless energy and enthusiasm

THE RAMBUNCTIOUS ROOSEVELTS

Roosevelt was a fond parent who loved roughhousing with his young sons. He insisted that of all of the families who had lived in the White House, none enjoyed their stay more than his did. Like an overgrown child himself at times, he took guests hiking through the grounds and sparred with boxing partners in the state rooms. His sons often played pranks on one another, and once, when Archie was sick with the measles, his brothers smuggled his favorite pony upstairs on the White House elevator.

Left: TR's sons Archie and Quentin, middle and right, enjoy themselves wrestling with their cousin Nicholas Roosevelt and their dog.

Above: Quentin Roosevelt seated on his Shetland pony on the White House lawn.

The president flashes his trademark toothy grin. He encouraged his children to lead active lives and loved playing with them, even joining them in pillow fights or starting football games on the White House lawn.

TR'S FOREIGN POLICY

Unlike his predecessors, Roosevelt believed that the United States needed to take a more active role in foreign affairs. He summed up his philosophy by advising, "Speak softly and carry a big stick." In 1907 he sent a "Great White Fleet" of navy ships on a worldwide goodwill tour, which also showed that the United States was capable of spanning the globe. In particular he wanted to impress the Japanese, who had recently bested the Russian fleet in the Pacific. He also deployed the army medical service to US foreign holdings—the Philippines, Guam, and Puerto Rico—to eliminate yellow fever and create a public health service.

The USS *Louisiana*, the flagship of the Great White Fleet. Postcards such as this one by the US Navy were popular with the public, who followed the fleet's journey around the globe.

COL. ROOSEVELT
Tells the story of
THE ROUGH RIDERS
in Scribner's Magazine. It begins in January and will run for six months, with many illustrations from photographs taken in the field.
JANUARY
SCRIBNER'S
NOW READY PRICE 25 CENTS

Magazine stories about his exploits as a Rough Rider during the Spanish-American War helped launch TR's political career.

> **"The one thing I want to leave my children is an honorable name."**
>
> —Theodore Roosevelt

THE PANAMA CANAL

As shipping grew more important to the American economy, it became critical to decrease the sailing distance between the East and West coasts of the United States—on average a 14,000-mile journey that included a dangerous trip around the tip of South America.

In 1880 the French had started to dig a canal along the 48-mile-wide Isthmus of Panama, but they were soon overwhelmed. When President Roosevelt aided Panama in gaining independence from Colombia, the new nation agreed to give the United States control of the French diggings. In 1904 engineers began work on one of the largest and most difficult construction projects ever undertaken. During the work more than 5,000 workers died from malaria and yellow fever and in landslides. Roosevelt, who was the first president to travel abroad while in office when he visited the site in 1906, had the original French equipment melted down and made into pins—a badge of merit for every person who helped build the canal.

The Panama Canal, which officially opened in 1914 with the merchant ship *Ancon* passing through its locks, shortened the journey from New York to San Francisco by 8,000 miles.

In 1908 *Judge* magazine depicted Roosevelt wearing an ornate crown symbolizing the Panama Canal, calling it "the greatest achievement for trade in modern times."

Timeline of the Roosevelt Presidency

US Events / **World Events**

1901 (World) Englishman C. Hubert Booth patents first powered vacuum cleaner

1901 (US) The first American Bowling Club tournament is held in Chicago

1901 (World) Guglielmo Marconi sends the first wireless transmissions across the Atlantic

1903 (US) Edwin Binney and C. Harold Smith produce the first box of Crayola crayons

1903 (US) Wright brothers fly *Flyer I* at Kitty Hawk, North Carolina

1903 (US) The Boston Red Sox win the first World Series, beating Pittsburgh five games to three.

1903 (US) Hershey builds a chocolate factory in Pennsylvania

1904–1905 (World) Russia and Japan are at war

1905 (World) German physicist Albert Einstein proposes Special Theory of Relativity

1908 (US) General Electric patents first electric toaster

1908 (US) J. C. Penney founds his chain of department stores

1908 (US) Children are reading *The Wind in the Willows* and *Anne of Green Gables*

27th President

William Howard Taft

"Big Bill"

1909–1913

William Howard Taft became president after a notable career in both the courtroom and the political arena. His love and respect for the law would remain a driving force throughout his life.

Taft was born in Cincinnati, Ohio, to a wealthy and well-regarded family. His father, Alphonso, was secretary of war under Grant. After graduating second in his class from Yale and attending Cincinnati Law School, Taft served in a series of increasingly important posts—including county prosecutor, Ohio superior court judge, and solicitor general for the United States. He also found time to court and marry his childhood sweetheart, Helen Herron.

In 1901 President William McKinley sent Taft to the Philippine Islands to organize a civilian government. Taft stayed on for two years as the country's first governor-general, at the request of the Filipino people.

In 1904 Theodore Roosevelt appointed him secretary of war and then four years later approved Taft as the Republican candidate for president. This was a mixed blessing: Roosevelt's popularity was undiminished when he left office, and Taft never came close to gaining his predecessor's level of public approval. It didn't help that Taft chose to push for a new federal tariff in 1909, a sticky issue that Roosevelt had managed to sidestep.

Filling TR's Shoes

Taft did follow in his mentor's footsteps as a trustbuster, launching 80 antitrust suits, including one against the country's industrial giant, US Steel. Unfortunately Roosevelt had approved the transaction in question, and now Taft found himself without the support of the former president or of big business. Taft, though well-intentioned, continued to drive away his allies, including the progressive Republicans, the antitrust reformers, and the conservationists.

During his term he strengthened the Interstate Commerce Commission and established both a postal savings bank and a parcel post system. Taft felt that the United States should invest in the countries of Latin America and Asia to help them grow, a foreign policy he referred to as "dollar diplomacy." Taft was also devoted to the cause of world peace; he believed that international arbitration could finally put an end to war.

"Politics makes me sick."

Eight years after Taft left office, Warren Harding named him chief justice of the Supreme Court. Even though he had been president, he considered this the high point of his career. After a fact-finding trip to visit the English parliament, he streamlined the Supreme Court, allowing it to prioritize cases and operate more efficiently. He was also responsible for the Supreme Court gaining its own home.

When Taft died in 1930, he became the first president to be buried in Arlington National Cemetery.

BIOGRAPHICAL FACTS

Birth September 15, 1857, Cincinnati, Ohio

Religion Unitarian

Education Yale College (graduated 1878); Cincinnati Law School

Occupation Lawyer; judge

Other Offices Ohio Superior Court; US solicitor general; US Circuit Court judge; governor of the Philippines; secretary of war; chief justice of the US Supreme Court

Political Party Republican

Vice President James S. Sherman

Age at Inauguration 51

Death March 8, 1930, Washington, DC

Even his supporters liked to poke fun at Taft's large girth, such as *Judge* magazine. Its 1906 cover labeled him "The Large-ical Candidate" for the 1908 election.

> "I think he has the most lovable personality I have ever come in contact with."
>
> —Theodore Roosevelt, about Taft

DID YOU KNOW...?

The Washington Monument framed by the Japanese cherry blossoms.

- Nellie Taft had the 3,000 Japanese cherry trees that still line the Tidal Basin planted there.
- Taft's cane, a gift from a geology professor, was made of 250,000-year-old wood.
- Taft weighed 300 pounds but enjoyed riding. Once, when he said he felt "good" after a ride, someone asked, "How's the horse?"
- Taft's son Robert was a US senator, and son Charles was mayor of Cincinnati. Grandson Robert Jr. was a senator, and great-grandson Robert A. Taft II was governor of Ohio.

Timeline of the Taft Presidency

US Events / **World Events**

1909 (US) National Association for the Advancement of Colored People (NAACP) formed in New York

1909 (World) Robert E. Peary reaches the North Pole

1909 (US) Congress authorizes an income tax

1910 (US) Author James MacGillivray publishes first stories of Paul Bunyon in the *Detroit News*

1910 (World) Halley's Comet makes an appearance

1910 (US) Boy Scouts established

1911 (US) Aviator Glenn Curtiss introduces the Triad seaplane, which can land on water

1912 (US) Oreo cookies introduced

1912 (World) Norwegian explorer Roald Amundsen is first to reach the South Pole

1912 (US) Fenway Park, home to the Boston Red Sox, opens

1912 (World) British ocean liner *Titanic* strikes iceberg and sinks

1913 (World) British editor Arthur Wynne invents the crossword puzzle

THE TAFT FAMILY

Father Alphonso Taft (1810–1891)

Occupation Lawyer; secretary of war

Mother Louisa Maria Torrey Taft (1827–1907)

Wife Helen Herron Taft

Birth June 2, 1861, Cincinnati, Ohio

Marriage June 19, 1886

Death May 22, 1943, Washington, DC

Children Robert Alphonso (1889–1953); Helen Herron (1891–1987); Charles Phelps (1897–1983)

William and Nellie Taft, seated, with their three children sitting in front, from left: Robert, Charley, and Helen.

The Supreme Court

During its first 145 years, the Supreme Court was homeless, moving from New York to Philadelphia to Washington as the nation's capital moved. In 1929 former president and then chief justice William Howard Taft persuaded Congress to authorize a permanent home. In 1935 the dignified Supreme Court Building opened its doors. An ornamental band that reads "Equal Justice Under Law" sits above the 16 marble columns at the west entrance.

The Supreme Court, the highest court in the country, represents the judiciary branch of the United States government. It rarely hears new cases; instead it serves as an appellate (appeals) court, reviewing and passing judgment on previously tried cases that have been appealed. Once the Supreme Court has ruled on a matter, its decision is final and cannot be appealed.

"Presidents come and go, but the Supreme Court goes on forever."

—William Howard Taft

More than 7,000 cases are filed with the court each year, but the Court rules on only a small number of them. The Court convenes on the first Monday of October and usually stays in session until the following June.

The Justices

The Supreme Court consists of eight associate justices presided over by a chief justice. A president appoints justices for life terms with the consent of the Senate. Justices can be removed only by retirement, resignation, or impeachment followed by conviction. Presidents typically choose justices with political viewpoints similar to their own, such as conservative, moderate, or liberal.

In most cases the chief justice has sworn in a new president. At left, Chief Justice John Marshall presides as Andrew Jackson takes the oath of office, March 4, 1829.

THE FIRST WOMAN JUSTICE

Associate Justice Sandra Day O'Connor

In 1981 President Ronald Reagan chose Arizona judge Sandra Day O'Connor to become the first female associate justice of the Supreme Court. Considered a moderate (neither liberal nor conservative) O'Connor often provided a critical "swing" vote in rulings. She served until 2006, when she retired. Ruth Bader Ginsburg, nominated by Bill Clinton in 1993, is the second woman to sit on the Supreme Court and is considered part of the "liberal wing."

As chief justice of the Supreme Court Taft was the only former president to swear in two new presidents, Calvin Coolidge and Herbert Hoover.

> "Whenever you put a man on the Supreme Court he ceases to be your friend."
>
> —Harry S. Truman

HISTORY OF THE COURT

The Supreme Court, established by the Constitution in 1787, first met on February 1, 1790, in New York City, the country's first capital. When Washington became the seat of government, the court moved its offices to the Capitol. In 1935 it relocated to its permanent home, a stately building with sweeping steps and tall marble columns.

Originally there were six justices, but as the country expanded, more were added. Under the earliest chief justices, John Jay (1789–1795), John Rutledge (1795), and Oliver Ellsworth (1796–1800), the court did not have the authority it would later acquire. Under John Marshall, however, the Supreme Court became the ultimate interpreter of the Constitution. This gave the Supreme Court the ability to overturn laws or executive actions it considered unconstitutional. As Alexander Hamilton wrote, "A constitution is, in fact, and must be regarded by the judges, as a fundamental law. It therefore belongs to them to ascertain its meaning." During the Marshall Court (1801–1836), justices also no longer issued rulings individually, but issued one ruling as a unit.

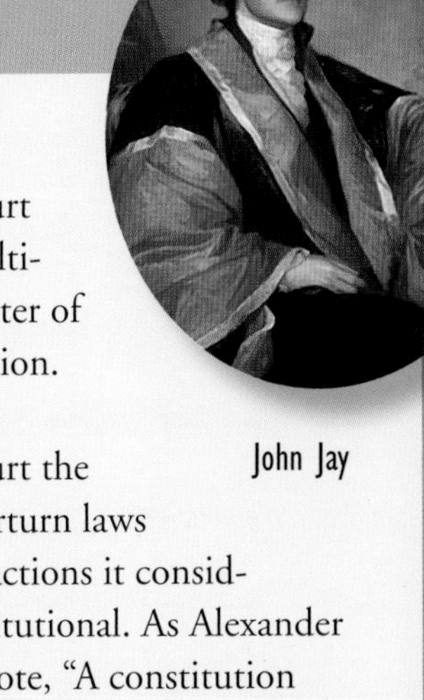

John Jay

Significant Rulings

Over the years the Supreme Court has made a number of historic decisions. Many of them changed the way Americans lived.

Marbury v. Madison

Marshall Court, 1803

This case created a special power called "judicial review," which allows the Supreme Court to judge whether decisions made by Congress follow the rules of the Constitution. This decision made the Court equal to the other two branches of government.

Dred Scott v. Sanford

Taney Court, 1857

Dred Scott, a slave, sued for his freedom after living in a state and a territory where slavery was illegal. The Court ruled seven to two against Scott, saying a slave was property and could not sue for freedom. The decision also barred anyone of African descent from becoming a US citizen.

Plessy v. Ferguson

Fuller Court, 1896

When Homer Adolph Plessy, who was one-eighth black, sat in a whites-only car on the East Louisiana Railroad, he was arrested. The court voted seven to one in favor of the Louisiana law, setting the standard of "separate but equal." This allowed for racial segregation but only if facilities for both races were of equal quality.

Brown v. Board of Education

Warren Court, 1954

It was a groundbreaking moment in civil rights history when the entire Court agreed that forcing children to attend separate schools based on the color of their skin was against the Constitution. It marked the end of "separate but equal."

Oregon v. Mitchell

Burger Court, 1970

This decision ruled that 18-year-olds can register to vote in state and federal elections.

Roe v. Wade

Burger Court, 1973

In a decision that still provokes debate, the Court ruled that abortion was a woman's constitutional right.

Bush v. Gore

Rehnquist Court, 2000

After the 2000 election, George W. Bush and Al Gore appeared tied. The results from the close Florida election would swing the decision. The Democrats requested a statewide vote recount, but the Supreme Court ruled five to four against it. The ruling ended all protests and declared that Bush had won enough votes in Florida to claim the presidency.

Woodrow Wilson

"Schoolmaster in Politics"

1913–1921

28th President

As a boy living in Georgia and South Carolina, Woodrow Wilson had seen firsthand the carnage of the Civil War. Yet he reluctantly led the country into a world war, declaring he would "make the world safe for democracy."

Wilson was born in 1856 in Staunton, Virginia, and lived in several other Southern states where his minister father was assigned. After graduating from the College of New Jersey (later called Princeton), he attended the University of Virginia Law School and Johns Hopkins University in Maryland, where he received his doctorate. As a promising young professor of political science, Wilson rose quickly, and by 1902 he was president of Princeton.

Wilson Takes Control

The conservative Democrats had their eye on Wilson as a prospective presidential candidate, and after he was elected governor of New Jersey in 1910, he proved his mettle by rising above party politics and introducing progressive reforms. He gained the presidential nomination in 1912 and won with 42 percent of the vote in a three-way race.

Wilson's first triumph was getting three key pieces of legislation through Congress—a lower tariff, a graduated income tax, and the Federal Reserve Act, which increased the nation's money supply. He also banished child labor and established an eight-hour day for railroad workers.

He narrowly won reelection in 1916, mostly for having kept the United States out of the war in Europe. But when German submarines began attacking American ships, he asked Congress to declare war on Germany, which it did on April 2, 1917. America rallied to the call, putting all its industrial might behind the war machine. Slowly the allied forces began to turn the tide. In 1918 Wilson appeared before Congress with his "Fourteen Points," listing his aims for the war and its aftermath. Last on the list was his plan for a "general association of nations" that would work together to maintain a peaceful coexistence.

"America was established not to create wealth but to realize a vision."

After the surrender of Germany in 1918, Wilson traveled to Paris to work on the peace arrangements. When he returned to Congress with the Versailles Treaty—which included the Covenant of the League of Nations, similar to today's United Nations—the Senate voted it down. Wilson set out on a nationwide tour to promote the treaty, even though his health was fragile. After he nearly died from a stroke, his second wife, Edith Bolling Galt, nursed him back to health—and some said took over the running of the country while he was ill.

Before he died in 1924, Wilson expressed a deep regret that the country's entry into the war had not resulted, as he'd hoped, in its becoming a member of the League of Nations.

BIOGRAPHICAL FACTS

Birth December 28, 1856, Staunton, Virginia
Religion Presbyterian
Education Princeton (graduated 1879)
Occupation Professor; lawyer
Other Offices Governor of New Jersey
Political Party Democratic
Vice President Thomas R. Marshall
Age at Inauguration 56
Death February 3, 1924, Washington, DC

A wartime poster for the American Red Cross. For his support of the relief organization, the Red Cross named Woodrow Wilson its first honorary president in 1913. Since then every chief executive has received this honor.

Ellen Wilson, third from left, with Jessie, Margaret, and Eleanor. The first lady was an accomplished artist.

Wilson throws out the first baseball on opening day in 1916. A keen baseball fan, he was the first sitting president to attend a World Series game. He never used his presidential pass for any of the games he went to; instead, he paid for them himself.

DID YOU KNOW...?

- Edith Wilson, Woodrow's second wife, could trace her ancestry back to Pocahontas.
- Wilson loved driving his 1919 Pierce-Arrow car with the top down.

THE WILSON FAMILY

Father Joseph Ruggles Wilson (1822–1903)
Occupation Presbyterian minister; professor of theology
Mother Jessie Janet Woodrow Wilson (1830–1888)
First Wife Ellen Axson Wilson (1860–1914)

The president with his first wife and their daughters. From left: Jessie, Woodrow, Ellen, Margaret, and Eleanor.

Marriage June 24, 1885
Children Margaret (1886–1944); Jessie (1887–1933); Eleanor (1889–1967)
Second Wife Edith Bolling Galt Wilson (1872–1961)
Marriage December 18, 1915

Timeline of the Wilson Presidency

US Events / **World Events**

1913 (World) Russian composer Igor Stravinsky debuts ballet *The Rite of Spring*

1914 (US) Charles Pajeau develops Tinker Toys

1914 (World) World War I begins as Germany invades Belgium

1914 (US) Scientist Robert Goddard patents multistage rocket and liquid rocket fuel

1915 (US) D. W. Griffith directs silent film classic *The Birth of a Nation*

1916 (World) German physicist Albert Einstein proposes General Theory of Relativity

1916 (US) John Lloyd Wright invents Lincoln Logs

1917 (World) Russian Revolution leads to formation of communist USSR

1917 (US) Military draft instated

1919 (World) Versailles Peace Treaty marks end to WWI

1920 (US) 18th Amendment prohibits production and sale of alcohol

1920 (US) 19th Amendment gives women the right to vote

Warren G. Harding

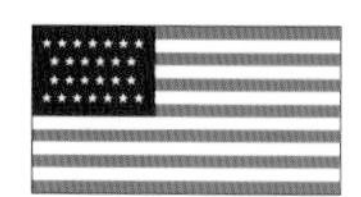

"President Hardly"

1921–1923

Fond of long-winded speeches and 50-cent words, Warren G. Harding brought a new prosperity to the postwar nation, until scandal and corruption shook the foundations of his presidency.

Harding was born near Marion, Ohio, the son of a doctor and a midwife. His father also owned a weekly newspaper, the *Argus*. After graduating from college, young Harding purchased his own newspaper, the *Marion Daily Star,* as a platform for his Republican beliefs. A war of words with a real estate investor sent the *Star*'s circulation soaring.

Harding suffered a nervous collapse in 1889 and entered a sanitarium for several weeks. In 1891 he married Florence Kling, the ambitious daughter of his local enemy. It was said she prodded him all the way to the White House. He soon embarked on a political career, serving as an Ohio senator, as lieutenant governor of Ohio, and then as US senator.

When the Republican presidential nomination became deadlocked in 1920, dark horse Harding emerged as the candidate after he assured the committee that there was nothing shady about his past. Harding neglected to tell them about his long-term girlfriend or his fondness for drink. With his platform promising a "return to normalcy"—and first-time women voters turning out to support him—Harding won in a landslide.

"Every student has the ability to be a successful learner."

Success and Scandal

Harding started out strong, cutting taxes, establishing the Bureau of Veterans Affairs, creating new immigration laws, lowering railroad rates, and promoting agriculture and a department of public welfare. He spoke out against lynching—the practice of killing African Americans without trial—and called for peacemaking in Europe.

The country seemed to be prospering under the popular president, but all was not rosy. Harding had given key federal posts to his old allies, called the "Ohio gang," and they were soon helping themselves to the government's money. Republican senator Albert Fall leased out a number of oil fields without competitive bidding—including one with a large boulder shaped like a teapot. The recipients of these leases gave Fall bribes amounting to the modern equivalent of four million dollars. The Teapot Dome scandal rocked the capital and came to represent Harding's presidency, even though it is unclear if he was aware of the corruption.

In June 1923 the president and the first lady set out on a "Voyage of Understanding," a nationwide tour aimed at rebuilding national confidence. While in San Francisco, Harding died of complications from pneumonia.

BIOGRAPHICAL FACTS

Birth November 2, 1865, Corsica, Ohio

Religion Baptist

Education Ohio Central College (graduated 1882)

Occupation Editor-publisher; businessman

Other Offices Ohio state senator; lieutenant governor of Ohio; US senator

Political Party Republican

Vice President Calvin Coolidge

Age at Inauguration 55

Death August 2, 1923, San Francisco, California

DID YOU KNOW...?

Harding and Laddie Boy tussle for a newsreel film.

- Harding was the first president to visit Alaska.
- His campaign was the first to be covered by newsreel footage.
- Harding's chiseled looks apparently attracted female voters, leading to the term "the Warren Harding effect" whenever a candidate succeeds mainly on appearance.

THE ORIGINAL "FIRST DOG"

Wildly popular with the public, Laddie Boy Harding was showered with gifts, including the photo of himself he poses with here.

Laddie Boy, the Hardings' playful Airedale terrier, was the first presidential pet to share the spotlight with his owners. Truly considered a member of the first family, Laddie Boy greeted and entertained White House guests, posed for the press and newsreel makers, and made public appearances.

THE HARDING FAMILY

Father George Tyron Harding (1843–1928)

Occupation Doctor; newspaper publisher

Mother Phoebe Elizabeth Dickerson Harding (1843–1910)

Wife Florence Kling De Wolfe Harding

Birth August 15, 1860, Marion, Ohio

Marriage July 8, 1891

Death November 21, 1924, Marion, Ohio

Occupation Piano teacher; newspaper publisher

After an unhappy first marriage, Florence Harding returned to her hometown and supported herself by giving piano lessons. She met Warren when she taught one of his brothers.

Timeline of the Harding Presidency

US Events	World Events
	1921 The parliament of newly formed Northern Ireland holds first elections
1921 Emergency Quota Act establishes quotas on immigration	
1921 Lie detector invented	
	1921 Researchers at the University of Toronto discover the hormone insulin
1922 First issue of *Reader's Digest* is published	
	1922 Tomb of King Tut discovered
1922 Jack Pressman creates a play doctor's bag when his children are afraid to visit the doctor. His company goes on to become the largest manufacturer of classic games	
	1923 Mexican revolutionary Pancho Villa is assassinated
1923 *Time* magazine hits newsstands for the first time	
	1923 Italy becomes world's first fascist state
1923 Yankee Stadium, "The House that Ruth Built," opens in the Bronx, New York	

Calvin Coolidge

"Silent Cal" **1923–1929**

He served during the "Roaring Twenties," but Calvin Coolidge brought a cautious conservatism to the White House after the corruption of the Harding years. He was content to let the country prosper around him, unaware that the United States would soon be facing financial disaster.

Coolidge, the only president born on the 4th of July, grew up in Plymouth, Vermont. He graduated with honors from Amherst College in western Massachusetts and, at his father's urging, remained in the area to practice law. He soon entered the political ring, and in spite of being a man of few words, he had a dry Vermont wit and was an inspiring speaker. And he had one other asset—a fun-loving wife, Grace Goodhue Coolidge, whose social skills nicely balanced his cool aloofness.

Coolidge doggedly moved up through the ranks of politics, serving in a number of local and state offices before successfully running for governor of Massachusetts in 1918. Two years later, the Republicans chose him as Harding's running mate after his no-nonsense handling of the Boston Police Strike gained him national recognition. When Harding died in office, Coolidge immediately initiated reforms, although he did retain Harding's cabinet. When more evidence of Harding-related corruption came to light, Coolidge managed to remain untarnished, and he gained the presidential nomination in 1924. Shortly after the nominating convention ended, his son Calvin Jr. died of blood poisoning. Coolidge continued to campaign in spite of his grief and easily won the popular vote.

A Term of His Own

Coolidge believed, as Jefferson had, that less government meant better government. As a strong supporter of American business, he cut taxes and also balanced the federal budget and reduced the national debt. He did not always address problems until they arose, which sometimes led to shortsighted policies. Unlike Wilson, he refused to support the League of Nations but did sign the Kellogg-Briand Pact, which condemned war as "an instrument" of international policy.

> **"Don't expect to build up the weak by pulling down the strong."**

Some critics claim that Coolidge's "hands-off" presidency set the stage for the Great Depression. Throughout his term Coolidge had encouraged investment in business and had refused to use the federal government to restrain the booming stock market. Whether or not he suspected that the country was about to enter a depression, he did not seek reelection, issuing a typically terse statement: "I do not choose to run for President in 1928."

After he left office, Coolidge completed his autobiography and wrote a syndicated newspaper column. He died of a heart attack in 1933.

BIOGRAPHICAL FACTS

Birth July 4, 1872, Plymouth, Vermont
Religion Congregationalist
Education Amherst College (graduated 1895)
Occupation Lawyer
Other Offices Massachusetts Legislature; mayor of Northampton, Massachusetts; lieutenant governor and governor of Massachusetts; vice president
Political Party Republican
Vice President Charles G. Dawes
Age at Inauguration 51
Death January 5, 1933, Northampton, Massachusetts

Grace Coolidge shows off one of her raccoons at the annual Easter Egg Roll. The animal-loving first lady kept numerous pets, including raccoons Rebecca and Reuben. She even included her white collie, Rob Roy, in her official portrait.

> "If you don't say anything, you won't be called on to repeat it."
>
> —Calvin Coolidge

DID YOU KNOW...?

John Coolidge administers the oath of office to his son Calvin at the Vermont family home.

- Coolidge was visiting his father when he learned of Harding's death. His father, a notary public, swore him in using the family Bible.
- Coolidge was the first vice president to sit in on cabinet meetings.
- "Keep Cool with Cal" was a popular campaign slogan
- Coolidge was the first president to have his inauguration broadcast on the radio.

THE COOLIDGE FAMILY

Father John Calvin Coolidge (1845–1926)
Occupation Storekeeper
Mother Victoria Josephine Moor Coolidge (1846–1885)
Wife Grace Anna Goodhue Coolidge
Birth January 3, 1879, Burlington, Vermont
Marriage October 4, 1905
Death July 8,1957, Northampton, Massachusetts
Children John (1906–2000); Calvin Jr. (1908–1924)

The Coolidges with son John and two of their dogs. Calvin Jr. died from blood poisoning from an infected blister that he developed while playing tennis.

Timeline of the Coolidge Presidency

US Events / **World Events**

1924 (World) A. A. Milne begins to write Winnie the Pooh stories

1924 (US) Citizenship Act grants citizenship to Native Americans

1924 (World) First Olympic Winter Games

1925 (US) Author F. Scott Fitzgerald publishes *The Great Gatsby*

1925 (World) Hitler publishes *Mein Kampf*

1925 (US) The Scopes (Monkey) Trial upholds law against the teaching of evolution in school

1926 (World) Gertrude Eberle swims the English Channel

1927 (US) Charles Lindbergh flies solo over the Atlantic

1927 (US) Great Mississippi Flood, worst Gulf Coast disaster until Hurricane Katrina

1927 (World) PEZ invented in Vienna, Austria, by Edward Haas III

1928 (World) British scientist Alexander Fleming discovers penicillin

1928 (US) Disney's Mickey Mouse appears in first sound cartoon

1928 (US) Bubblegum invented

Herbert C. Hoover

"The Great Engineer" **1929–1933**

Though Herbert Hoover was a renowned humanitarian and a brilliant engineer, his presidency suffered from his lack of political experience, especially when faced with the effects of the Great Depression.

He was born in Iowa and orphaned at the age of eight. Quaker relatives raised him, and he went on to graduate from Stanford University with a degree in engineering. After he married his college sweetheart, Lou Henry, the couple traveled to China, where he became the country's leading engineer. At the outbreak of the Boxer Rebellion, an uprising against foreign influence, he and Lou found themselves trapped for a month inside the war zone. Lou helped out in the local hospital, while he oversaw the building of barricades and even risked his life to rescue a group of Chinese children.

When the United States entered World War I, Woodrow Wilson made Hoover head of the Food Administration. Hoover managed to keep the overseas troops fed without instituting rationing at home. After the war he arranged shipments of food for the millions who were starving in Europe.

When Coolidge chose not to run again in 1928, the Republicans turned to Hoover, who had been his secretary of commerce. "Coolidge prosperity" seemed likely to continue under Hoover, but in October 1929 the stock market crashed, plunging the nation into a severe economic depression. Within a few years the great engine of American industry had ground almost to a halt.

America's Dark Days

Even as a drought in the Midwest made the situation worse, Hoover seemed to take his time reacting to the Depression. In 1931 he presented a program to Congress that would aid businesses and farmers facing the loss of their land to foreclosure. He also asked for banking reforms and loans to the states for feeding the poor. He signed an act creating the first federal unemployment assistance and tried to stimulate the economy with increased public works. At the same time he declared that caring for the multitudes who were out of work was not a federal problem but the responsibility of local governments and volunteer organizations. His opponents in Washington began to label him "callous and cruel."

"About the time we think we can make ends meet, somebody moves the ends."

Hoover lost the election of 1932 to Franklin D. Roosevelt, and for years he was critical of his successor's New Deal policy. Presidents Truman and Eisenhower both appointed him to head commissions that sharply cut federal spending.

Hoover remained active well into old age and was 90 years old when he died in 1964.

BIOGRAPHICAL FACTS

Birth August 10, 1874, West Branch, Iowa

Religion Quaker

Education Stanford University (graduated 1895)

Occupation Engineer

Other Offices Secretary of commerce; chairman of Commission for Relief in Belgium; US Food Administrator; chairman of Supreme Economic Council; secretary of commerce

Political Party Republican

Vice President Charles Curtis

Age at Inauguration 54

Death October 20, 1964, New York, New York

Lou Hoover dressed in her uniform as president of the Girl Scouts of America. An avid supporter of scouting, she made regular radio broadcasts, most of them encouraging the nation's youth to live active lives.

Hoover with King Tut, one of his German shepherds. King Tut shared the president's home with eight other dogs—and an opossum.

DID YOU KNOW . . . ?

- Hoover was the first Quaker president.
- Coolidge, with his Vermont drawl, referred to Hoover as "wonduh boy."
- He was the first president born west of the Mississippi River.
- Lou Hoover was Stanford University's first female geology student.
- Hoover Dam, one of the greatest engineering projects in history, was named for him.

"Children are our most valuable natural resource."

—Herbert Hoover

THE HOOVER FAMILY

Father Jesse Clark Hoover (1846–1880)

Occupation Blacksmith; shopkeeper

Mother Hulda Randall Minthorn Hoover (1849–1883)

Wife Lou Henry Hoover

Birth March 29, 1874, Waterloo, Iowa

Marriage February 10, 1899

Death January 7, 1944, New York, New York

Children Herbert (1903–1969); Allan (1907–1993)

Poster for Hoover's Children's Relief Committee. During and after World War I, the Hoovers worked to organize aid to war-torn Europe.

Timeline of the Hoover Presidency

US Events	World Events
1929 First Academy Awards	
1929 New York stock market crashes	
	1929 Canada and America agree on plan to preserve Niagara Falls
1929 Donald Duncan popularizes the yo-yo in the United States	
	1930 Mohandas Gandhi organizes civil disobedience in India to protest British rule
1930 The 3M Company first markets Scotch Tape	
	1930 Pluto discovered
1931 "The Star-Spangled Banner" is adopted as national anthem	
	1931 Christ monument built on Rio de Janeiro hilltop
	1931 The Chinese Soviet Republic proclaimed by Mao Zedong
1932 Amelia Earhart is first woman to fly solo across the Atlantic	
	1932 Ole Christiansen begins to manufacture Lego toy blocks
1932 Scientists split the atom	
	1932 Loch Ness monster first spotted

Franklin D. Roosevelt

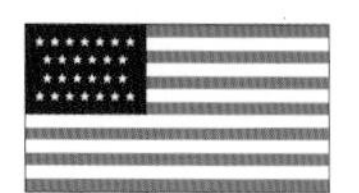

"FDR"

1933–1945

Franklin D. Roosevelt was a man of contrasts—a son of privilege who defended the poor, an athlete struck down by a crippling disease. Even his well-bred features seemed at odds with his jutting, businesslike chin. He battled back from his infirmity to become a four-term president, and not only led the country out of the Depression but also through a devastating global war.

Roosevelt's parents were both from old New York families, and he grew up among the social elite. The headmaster at Groton, his boarding school, encouraged students to help the poor by entering public service, a lesson Roosevelt never forgot. He graduated from Harvard, and in 1902 he met his future wife Eleanor Roosevelt, Theodore's niece, at a White House reception.

In 1910 Roosevelt, who was working as a corporate lawyer, was elected to the state legislature. President Wilson appointed him assistant secretary of the navy in 1914, where he quickly learned to negotiate with Congress to get his budgets passed. Seven years later he was struck down by what seemed to be polio, which left him crippled for life. Many believed that his political career was over.

But Roosevelt knew he belonged in the political arena, and in 1928 New Yorkers elected him as governor. When Hoover seemed incapable of resolving the Great Depression, the country swept him out of office in 1932 and voted in Roosevelt by a healthy margin. Roosevelt had promised the people a "new deal" and quickly worked to make good on that vow. During his first hundred days, he enacted a recovery program to relieve the 13 million unemployed Americans and to aid business and agriculture. By 1935 the United States was beginning its slow recovery.

Drawn into a World War

Roosevelt had established a "good neighbor" policy with US allies, agreeing to provide support against any aggressors. Yet he tried to keep the nation neutral after war broke out in Europe in 1939. When Germany invaded France and launched an assault on England, Roosevelt did everything he could to aid the British short of military intervention. But when the Japanese bombed Pearl Harbor, Hawaii, in December 1941, Roosevelt had no choice but to declare war. Soon after, Italy and Germany declared war on the United States. The nation rallied, turning the might of America's industrial war machine against its enemies on three continents.

"The only thing we have to fear is fear itself."

As the war wound down, Roosevelt looked to the future, imagining a league called the United Nations that would maintain world peace. He died of a cerebral hemorrhage before his inspired vision could become a reality. He was later named the foremost political leader of the 20th century.

BIOGRAPHICAL FACTS

Birth January 30, 1882, Hyde Park, New York

Religion Episcopalian

Education Harvard University (graduated 1903); Columbia Law School

Occupation Lawyer

Other Offices Member of New York State Legislature; assistant secretary of the navy; governor of New York

Political Party Democrat

Vice President John Nance Garner; Henry A. Wallace; Harry S. Truman

Age at Inauguration 51

Death April 12, 1945, Warm Springs, Georgia

FDR campaigning for vice president in 1920.

FDR at age 12 with his mother, Sara Delano Roosevelt. FDR lived a sheltered childhood on his wealthy family's estate in Hyde Park, New York. Sara was a forceful woman, who according to Eleanor wanted "to direct his every thought and deed."

Eleanor Roosevelt casts her vote in the elections of 1936. Although shy and awkward as a young woman, Eleanor was a charming and self-assured first lady. Transforming the role from "hostess" to "ambassador," she tirelessly traveled the country, gave lectures and radio broadcasts, and wrote a newspaper column called "My Day."

DID YOU KNOW . . . ?

- Recent studies indicate FDR's illness was not polio, but more likely Guillain-Barré syndrome.
- FDR appointed the first woman to the cabinet, Secretary of Labor Frances Perkins, and the first woman as US ambassador to a foreign country, Ruth Bryan, minister to Denmark.
- He was the first president whose mother was eligible to vote for him.
- FDR was distantly related on his mother's side to Laura Ingalls Wilder, author of *Little House on the Prairie*.
- In office longer than any other president, FDR served three terms and died during his fourth.
- FDR's favorite food was fried cornmeal mush.
- Swimming was his favorite sport.

THE ROOSEVELT FAMILY

Father James Roosevelt (1828–1900)

Occupation Lawyer; financier

Mother Sara Delano Roosevelt (1854–1941)

Wife Anna Eleanor Roosevelt

Birth October 11, 1884, New York, New York

Marriage March 17, 1905

Death November 7, 1962, New York, New York

Children Anna Eleanor (1906–1975); James (1907–1991); Elliott (1910–1990); Franklin Delano Jr. (1914–1988); John Aspinwall (1916–1981)

Eleanor and four of her children in 1920, with their dog Chief. From left: Elliott, John, Franklin Jr., and Anna.

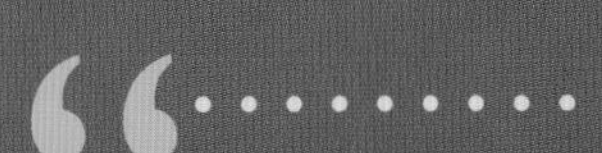

It is not fair to ask of others what you are unwilling to do yourself."

—Eleanor Roosevelt

THE FOUR FREEDOMS

FDR's 1941 State of the Union Address is often called the "Four Freedoms Speech." As the United States geared itself to enter the war already raging across Europe and the Pacific, the president sought to rally Americans to the cause. He listed four fundamental freedoms that everyone, "everywhere in the world," had the right to claim:

- Freedom of speech and expression
- Freedom of religion
- Freedom from want
- Freedom from fear

The Roosevelt Memorial includes a statue of FDR's Scottish terrier, Fala. Fala was a celebrity in his own right and had a social secretary to answer fan mail. He is buried in the Rose Garden at Hyde Park, near FDR.

THE NEW DEAL

When he was elected, FDR promised the nation a "new deal" to combat the Depression. It was his goal to "discipline" business and give aid to the needy and the elderly. He delivered on his promise with a series of programs of "relief, reform, and recovery" that would rebuild the economy and revitalize the people. Among his dozens of "alphabet" agencies were the Securities and Exchange Commission (SEC), Federal Deposit Insurance Corporation (FDIC), the Federal Housing Administration (FHA), and the Tennessee Valley Authority (TVA)—all still in operation, along with his Social Security System.

With 13 million Americans out of work, FDR knew that jobs had to be created for the country to get back on its feet. In 1935 he instituted the Works Progress Administration (WPA), which employed millions of women and men, especially those in rural areas. This massive civilian task force built roads, public buildings, airports, dams, and bridges and operated programs devoted to stimulating the arts and increasing literacy. The WPA also distributed food and clothing, arranged for housing, and fed children. When the WPA ended in 1943, when workers were needed for the war effort, it formed the largest employment base in the country.

Poster advertising the WPA Federal Writers' Project illustrated guide to natural history.

ELEANOR AND FRANKLIN

When the couple first married, Eleanor was shy and retiring, a social wallflower compared to her dynamic, handsome husband, Franklin. She preferred to remain out of the public spotlight and raise their children. But when Franklin fell ill, she became his lifeline, encouraging him in his battle to walk again and supporting his return to politics. As first lady, she gave press conferences, lectures, and radio broadcasts, and traveled the country as an ambassador of the White House. Although she knew of Franklin's affairs with other women, she remained at his side. After his death she became the American spokesperson in the United Nations and by the end of her life had become one of the most beloved women in the world.

Eleanor and Franklin, looking happy, in 1905, the year they were married.

Fireside Chat, September 1941. To calm the fears of Americans, during his years as president FDR made 30 of these radio addresses on topics of national concern. In the 1930s and '40s, nearly every home had a radio, so it was the most direct way to reach a wide audience.

> **"They had the most separate relationship I have ever seen between man and wife. And the most equal."**
>
> —J. B. West, on the Roosevelts

ROOSEVELT AND CHURCHILL

During World War II, FDR and Great Britain's prime minister, Winston Churchill, forged a successful political alliance as well as a warm friendship. Together they determined the military strategies that would eventually defeat Nazi Germany. Near the end of the European war, they met with Soviet leader Joseph Stalin at a conference in the resort town of Yalta. In return for Soviet aid in the Pacific war, the Allied leaders reluctantly allowed Stalin to take control of Poland with the understanding that there would be free elections. After a rigged election, Poland became a socialist state. Communism would soon expand throughout Eastern Europe, creating a climate of political tension that resulted in the Cold War.

Churchill and Roosevelt at the Yalta summit meeting in 1945.

FDR AND THE PRESS

A rare photo of FDR in his wheelchair, with his constant companion, Fala, and a young visitor at Hyde Park.

As a result of his illness, FDR used a wheelchair in private, but in public he made sure he always appeared standing upright. He understood that some people might equate his physical limitations with the inability to be a strong leader. The press of that time was less intrusive—and perhaps more respectful of its leaders—than it is today, and they agreed not to reveal his secret. There are very few photos of FDR in his wheelchair, and when he was photographed with one of his sons or an aide at his side, the public did not know that the men were keeping him steady on his feet.

> **"Meeting Franklin Roosevelt was like opening your first bottle of champagne; knowing him was like drinking it."**
>
> —WINSTON CHURCHILL

Eleanor in 1949, with a poster of the Universal Declaration of Human Rights. She went on to become an accomplished author, speaker, and advocate of civil rights. Truman appointed her as a delegate to the UN General Assembly from 1945 to 1952, where she chaired the committee that drafted and approved the declaration.

Timeline of the Roosevelt Presidency

US Events / **World Events**

1933 (World) Adolf Hitler becomes the chancellor of Germany; first Nazi concentration camp

1934 (US) Massive dust storms on the Great Plains spark migration by farmers to California

1935 (US) Monopoly hits stores

1936 (World) The Spanish Civil War begins

1937 (World) Japan invades China

1939 (US) Judy Garland stars in *The Wizard of Oz*

1939 (World) Germany invades Poland, opening World War II

1939 (US) Black opera singer Marian Anderson performs at the Lincoln Memorial

1941 (World) Japan bombs Pearl Harbor; Germany and Italy declare war on the United States

1942 (US) Debut of Little Golden Books for children

1942 (US) Roosevelt orders internment of Japanese Americans

1943 (US) Slinky makes world debut

1944 (World) D-Day landings on Normandy beaches in France begin the liberation of Western Europe

Cold War Presidents

The formation of an ominous mushroom cloud from the second atomic bomb explosion, on Nagasaki, Japan, which brought an end to World War II. After the war, the threat of nuclear destruction framed the contest between the United States and the Soviet Union, known as the Cold War.

The Cold War was the period of global tension that arose after World War II. It pitted the United States and its democratic allies against the Soviet Union and the other Communist countries of Europe and Asia. It's called a "cold" war because it usually involved political strategy and military maneuvering rather than open fighting.

Communism arose in Russia in 1917, when the Russian Revolution replaced the monarchy with a form of government that would distribute wealth evenly to the workers. By the end of World War II, the Union of Soviet Socialist Republics, or USSR, emerged as a world power.

"Let us not be deceived—we are today in the midst of a cold war."

—FINANCIER BERNARD BARUCH, 1947

Soviet leader Joseph Stalin had been a US ally, but after the war ended he placed most of Eastern Europe under a dictatorship. This "Soviet bloc" acted as a barrier against any aggression toward Russia, especially from the United States with its atomic bomb. Winston Churchill declared that "an iron curtain" had descended over the area.

America and other free nations considered communism a repressive form of government and a threat to world peace. Yet it appealed to many undeveloped nations because it promised, though rarely delivered, an equal share to all workers. In 1947 the Truman Doctrine offered financial aid to any country at risk of falling to communism. Still, by the early 1950s communism had spread to China and North Korea. Under President Truman, America entered into war to defend South Korea from an invasion by North Korea.

When the United States dropped two atomic bombs on Japan, the concept of traditional warfare gave way to the threat of massive destruction raining from the sky. Not only did atomic weapons destroy cities, they also left behind deadly radioactive fallout, which the wind could carry great distances. Now both world powers began to escalate their military strength, hoping that a show of force would prevent the other side from striking first, thus creating a "balance of terror."

During the 1950s, Americans grew increasingly fearful of a possible Russian attack, building bomb shelters in their backyards and teaching schoolchildren to "duck and cover" under their desks. This blind fear of communism led to Senate hearings presided over by Senator Joseph McCarthy, who believed it was his mission to root out Communists who had infiltrated the government as well as the entertainment industry and the arts. Anyone even suspected of Communist sympathies was "blacklisted," and many people unfairly lost their jobs during this witch-hunt.

When the Russians launched *Sputnik*, the first artificial satellite, the United States scrambled to catch up, fearing that space might become a future battlefield. The National Aeronautics and Space Administration (NASA) began to compete with Russian scientists to see who would win the "space race." The Russians sent the first human into space, but America triumphed by landing the first humans on the moon.

Cold War Turns to Real War

In 1962 the two countries came close to outright war during the Cuban Missile Crisis, but although tensions continued between the two nations, they never again escalated to that point.

In the early 1960s things began heating up in Southeast Asia. When Communist North Vietnam made an attempt to take over South Vietnam, American Special Forces were sent to train soldiers for the South. This "police action" escalated into a war and, in 1965 thousands of American troops were deployed to stop the spread of communism. By the end of President Johnson's administration, it was clear that the war was not going well. Anti-war demonstrators took to the streets, and young men burned their draft cards in protest. Nixon ended the war by pulling out the remaining US troops in 1973, and South Vietnam fell to the North.

By the 1970s more enlightened leadership in the Soviet Union and Red China led to a relaxing of open hostility called "detente." During the administration of George H. W. Bush, the Berlin Wall came down, reuniting Germany and officially signaling the end of the Cold War.

WHAT DOES THAT MEAN?

Blacklisting Boycotting or punishing people with unpopular beliefs

Communism A political doctrine that supports government ownership of all industry, with the profits distributed to the masses. Private ownership of property is outlawed

Iron Curtain The real and symbolic barriers of Communist countries of Eastern Europe,that separated them from the West

Red Term (taken from the color of the blood of the working class) used to indicate Communist affiliation, as in "Red Army." American Communist sympathizers were called "pinkos"

THE BATTLE FOR BERLIN

World War II divided Germany: the Allies occupied the West, and the Soviets occupied the East. Berlin, in the East, was similarly divided. The free world wanted a strong, democratic Germany and set about rebuilding West Germany. Most East Germans could not see how the West was prospering, but East Berliners saw first-hand how well their neighbors were doing. The Soviets, angered by this proof of capitalism outperforming communism, wanted the Allies gone. When Stalin cut off all supply lines to West Berlin, the Allies airlifted supplies to the city for 11 months until the Soviets ended the blockade. Still, skilled East Berliners continued to seek job opportunities in West Berlin, so in 1961 the Soviets erected a barrier between the two sectors: first barbed wire and then a concrete wall with guard towers. The wall became a stark reminder of Soviet repression.

33rd President

Harry S. Truman

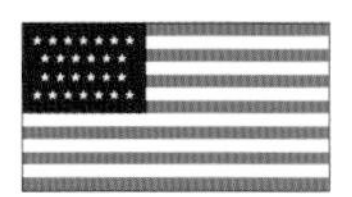

"The Man of Independence"

1945–1953

A sign on Harry Truman's desk read "The buck stops here," expressing his belief that it was the president's job to make tough decisions. Soon after he inherited a nation at war, Truman made a truly difficult decision that would end the conflict —and signal the start of the Atomic Age.

Truman was born in Lamar, Missouri, and grew up in Independence, a fitting hometown for a man who usually went his own way. He worked as a farmer for more than a decade and then served in France during World War I. After the war he married Elizabeth "Bess" Wallace and opened a haberdashery, or men's accessories store, in Kansas City. Always active in the Democratic Party, he became a county court judge in 1922 and in 1936 took a seat in the US Senate. In the 1940s, as head of a Senate committee investigating wartime waste and corruption, Truman saved the country an estimated $15 billion.

Roosevelt chose Truman as running mate for his fourth term, but the two men had not yet conferred on state matters when Roosevelt died. At first Truman knew nothing of the secret atomic bomb experiments in New Mexico or of FDR's concerns over the threat of Soviet Russia. The war in Europe was over, but the weakened Japanese refused all pleas to surrender. To end the war, Truman ordered the dropping of atomic bombs on Hiroshima and Nagasaki, two cities with war-related industries. Japan immediately surrendered.

From New Deal to Fair Deal

The United States had established itself as a world power, and Truman now turned to stimulating a peacetime economy. He submitted a program of "Twenty-one points" to Congress, which included expanding Social Security and the Fair Employment Practices Act and advocated the construction of public housing and slum clearance. The program became known as the Fair Deal and symbolized to Truman that he had become, as he put it, president "in my own right."

"All my life, whenever it comes time to make a decision, I make it and forget about it."

Truman also proved himself a capable foreign policy administrator. The Truman Doctrine gave aid to countries at risk from Communist takeover, and the Marshall Plan, named for his secretary of state, enabled war-torn Europe to make a remarkable recovery. Truman ordered tons of supplies airlifted to Berlin when the Russians blockaded parts of the city, and he was instrumental in negotiating an alliance among the nations of the West, which came to be called the North Atlantic Treaty Organization, or NATO.

In 1950 America successfully went to war to prevent Communist North Korea from invading South Korea. Still, the specter of communism would haunt America for several long decades.

BIOGRAPHICAL FACTS

Birth May 8, 1884, Lamar, Missouri
Religion Baptist
Education University of Kansas City Law School
Occupation Farmer; haberdasher
Other Offices Judge on Jackson County Court; US senator; vice president
Military Service Captain in 35th Infantry Division
Political Party Democratic
Vice President Alben W. Barkley
Age at Inauguration 60
Death December 26, 1972, Kansas City, Missouri

Harry and Bess Truman's wedding day, June 28, 1919. Harry's middle initial didn't stand for anything; he just liked the sound of it.

Painting of the Trumans' daughter, Margaret, by Greta Kempton. Margaret pursued a singing career during her father's presidency. Years later, after marrying Clifton Daniel and having four sons, she launched a successful writing career and penned a popular series of mysteries set in Washington.

THE FAMOUS SIGN

A sign that sat on President Truman's desk in his White House office for much of his administration read "The Buck Stops Here." The saying derives from the slang expression "pass the buck,"

which means passing responsibility on to someone else. As holder of the nation's highest office, Truman knew that it was his job to make the tough decisions—and accept the responsibility for them. In his farewell address of 1953, he said, "The President—whoever he is—has to decide. He can't pass the buck to anybody. No one else can do the deciding for him. That's his job."

THE TRUMAN FAMILY

Father John Anderson Truman (1851–1914)
Occupation Farmer
Mother Martha Ellen Young Truman (1852–1947)
Wife Elizabeth "Bess" Virginia Wallace Truman
Birth February 13, 1885, Independence, Missouri
Marriage June 28, 1919
Death October 18, 1982, Independence, Missouri
Children Mary Margaret (1924–2008)

Bess Truman. The first lady valued her privacy and often put off reporters with "No comment."

Timeline of the Truman Presidency

US Events / **World Events**

1945 (World) Atomic bombs dropped on Hiroshima and Nagasaki

1947 (US) Jackie Robinson, first black major-league baseball player, signs with Brooklyn Dodgers

1947 (World) India gains independence from Great Britain

1948 (US) Racial segregation ends in the armed forces

1948 (World) Israel writes its declaration of independence

1949 (US) First Volkswagen Beetle arrives in the US from Germany. No one is interested—yet

1949 (US) Silly Putty hits the toy market

1949 (World) The Soviet Union tests its first atomic bomb, code named "Joe I"

1950 (US) Charles Schulz's comic strip *Peanuts* first appears in newspapers

1950 (World) Mother Teresa begins her charity work in Calcutta, India

1951 (US) Colorforms are first manufactured

1952 (US) Mr. Potato Head is the first toy advertised on television

Dwight D. Eisenhower

"Ike"

1953–1961

Comparisons between Dwight Eisenhower and Ulysses Grant are unavoidable: both were West Point graduates and victorious commanders, and both had no political experience prior to becoming president. Unlike Grant the conservative Eisenhower suffered no scandals, and he kept the country prospering while he navigated through the treacherous waters of Cold War politics.

Eisenhower was born in Texas to a deeply religious, middle-class family. An excellent athlete, he began a military career after graduating from West Point. While stationed in Texas he met his wife, Mamie Doud. Although he never saw combat, Eisenhower was a skilled tank crew instructor during World War I. This duty was followed by staff service under legendary generals John J. Pershing and Douglas MacArthur.

At the outbreak of World War II, the army sent him to Washington to advise on war plans and tactics. Within two years Eisenhower rose to the rank of Supreme Allied Commander Europe. He commanded the invasion of North Africa in 1942, and on D-Day—June 6, 1944—he masterminded the mass landing of American and British troops in France, the largest amphibious assault in history.

After Allied victories over both Germany and Japan, Ike was hailed as a hero and in 1951 was named supreme commander of the new NATO forces. When Democrat Truman decided not to seek another term, the Republicans convinced Eisenhower to run. He won in a landslide.

From General to Cold Warrior

Eisenhower negotiated a truce with North Korea, leaving troops along the border to ensure peace. After Stalin died, the new Soviet leaders agreed to meet with Eisenhower and his European allies in Geneva. Since both America and Russia had developed hydrogen bombs, it was critical to reach an accord. Although the Russians did not agree to a mutual exchange of military plans, their relaxed attitude at the summit eased tensions.

"History does not long entrust the care of freedom to the weak or the timid."

After he recuperated from a heart attack, voters elected Ike to a second term, during which he continued to support both New Deal and Fair Deal policies. Although he worked to maintain world peace, he also created an interstate highway system for strategic military purposes. When the Supreme Court ordered school desegregation, he sent troops to Little Rock, Arkansas, to enforce the ruling. He also integrated the armed forces.

Eisenhower died in 1969. His presidency was marked by a national conservatism in clothing, the arts, and in attitudes, but the new decade would soon be "rocked" by a powerful youth movement.

BIOGRAPHICAL FACTS

Birth October 14, 1890, Denison, Texas
Religion Presbyterian
Education US Military Academy in West Point, N.Y. (graduated 1915)
Occupation Soldier
Military Service Army chief of staff; Supreme Commander of Allied Forces in Europe
Political Party Republican
Vice President Richard M. Nixon
Age at Inauguration 62
Death March 28, 1969, Washington, DC

Dwight, in his army uniform, and Mamie on their wedding day in July 1916.

Mamie Eisenhower chose a pink silk gown sprinkled with rhinestones for the 1953 inaugural balls. The popular first lady was known for her ultra-feminine style, and the color "Mamie pink" was her signature color.

DID YOU KNOW . . . ?

- His campaign slogan, "I like Ike," became one of the most popular in US politics.
- Ike's mother was a pacifist who locked his military books in the attic.
- Eisenhower loved to paint in oils and watercolor in his spare time.
- He ordered the White House squirrels to be trapped and relocated when they interfered with his golf putts.

I LIKE IKE

"Peace and justice are two sides of the same coin."

—Dwight Eisenhower

THE EISENHOWER FAMILY

Father David Jacob Eisenhower (1863–1942)
Occupation Mechanic
Mother Ida Elizabeth Stover Eisenhower (1862–1946)
Wife Marie "Mamie" Geneva Doud Eisenhower
Birth November 14, 1896, Boone, Iowa
Marriage July 1, 1916
Death November 1, 1979, Washington, DC
Children Doud Dwight (1917–1921); John Sheldon Doud (b. 1923)

Christmas 1957. Mamie walks hand in hand with grandchildren David and Mary Jean. Barbara and John Eisenhower follow, while the president ushers granddaughters Barbara and Susan.

Timeline of the Eisenhower Presidency

US Events	World Events
	1953 Biologist and physician Jonas Salk announces polio vaccine
1953 The first Chevrolet Corvette rolls off Detroit assembly line	
	1954 British athlete Roger Bannister runs the first four-minute mile
1954 A Memphis radio station plays the first Elvis Presley record	
1955 Rosa Parks refuses to give up her bus seat to a white person	
	1956 Pakistan becomes the first Islamic republic
1956 Play-Doh enters the market as wallpaper cleaner	
1956 Yankee Don Larsen pitches only perfect game in World Series	
	1956 Suez Crisis: Israel invades Egypt's Sinai Peninsula
1957 Wham-O produces the Frisbee	
	1957 Soviets launch *Sputnik I*, the first space satellite
1958 First US satellite, *Explorer I*, is launched into orbit	
1959 Mattel debuts the Barbie doll	
	1959 Second Vatican Council

John F. Kennedy

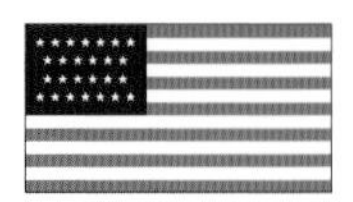

"The King of Camelot" **1961–1963**

John F. Kennedy's youthful energy and progressive politics, including programs for minorities and the poor, brought renewed hope to many Americans. Sadly the promise of his presidency was cut short by assassination.

Kennedy was born into a wealthy Massachusetts family, to a father with political aspirations for his sons. He graduated from Harvard and then served in the navy aboard a PT (patrol torpedo) boat in the Pacific. When a Japanese destroyer rammed his boat, Kennedy was seriously injured. In spite of this, he managed to help his crew to safety.

After the war ended he returned to the Boston area and worked as a journalist before his election to Congress. In 1953 he became a senator and that same year married a stylish young debutante, Jacqueline Bouvier. In 1960 the Democrats chose him to run against Vice President Richard Nixon. In a series of televised debates, Kennedy's vigor and rugged good looks overshadowed Nixon, who appeared pasty and uneasy on camera. The election was extremely close, but Kennedy won, becoming the nation's first Roman Catholic president.

Inspiring a Generation

After delivering a stirring inaugural address, which challenged citizens to "Ask not what your country can do for you, but what you can do for your country," Kennedy set in motion America's longest economic expansion since World War II. He supported new civil rights legislation; developed youth programs with international outreach, such as the Peace Corps; and worked to end the cycle of poverty and crime that afflicted the inner cities. He was also an advocate of the arts, considering them a vital part of a nation's culture.

"For of those to whom much is given, much is required."

Kennedy's victories at home did not guarantee easy relations with the Soviets. When a group of US-backed Cuban exiles failed in an attempt to invade communist Cuba at the Bay of Pigs, Kennedy suffered his first real setback. The Soviets, no doubt made bold by Kennedy's failed Cuban strategy, increased pressure against West Berlin. Kennedy countered by building up West German military strength. After erecting the Berlin Wall, the Russians eased hostilities in Europe for a time.

In 1962 Kennedy successfully confronted the Soviets over missile bases being built in Cuba. He truly believed that the Russians did not desire a nuclear war, and in 1963 he negotiated a landmark test ban treaty with them. Kennedy was just beginning to see the realization of his goal, "a world of law and free choice, banishing the world of war and coercion," when he was assassinated in Dallas. The nation staggered at the news, and many people still recall where they were the moment they heard their vital, young president had died.

BIOGRAPHICAL FACTS

Birth May 29, 1917, Brookline, Massachusetts

Religion Roman Catholic

Education Harvard (graduated 1940)

Occupation Reporter; author

Other Offices Member of US House of Representatives; US Senator

Lieutenant Kennedy aboard PT 109 during his World War II service.

Military Service Lieutenant, Naval Reserve (active duty 1941–1945)

Political Party Democratic

Vice President Lyndon B. Johnson

Age at Inauguration 43

Death November 22, 1963, Dallas, Texas

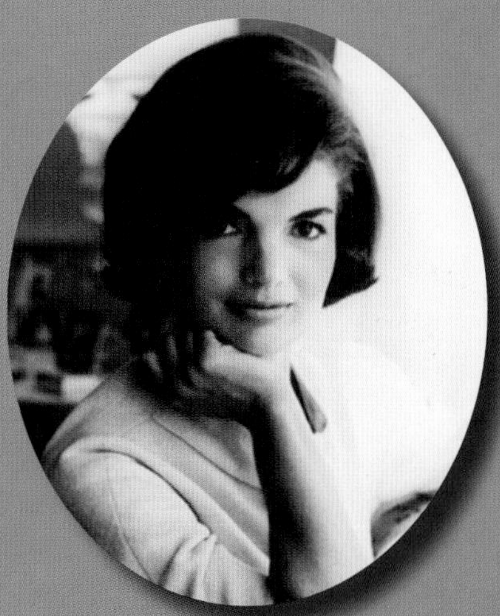

As first lady, Jacqueline Kennedy was one of the most photographed women in the world.

"For time and the world do not stand still. Change is the law of life. And those who look only to the past or the present are certain to miss the future."

—John F. Kennedy

The president and first lady greet a guest at a reception in 1962. The stylish couple brought a sense of youth and glamour to the White House.

CAMELOT: "ONE BRIEF SHINING MOMENT"

During Kennedy's administration, there was a popular Broadway play about King Arthur called *Camelot*. Kennedy loved to listen to the music from the show, especially one song with the line, "don't let it be forgot, that once there was a spot, for one brief shining moment, that was known as Camelot." This ideal vision of a perfect world inspired Kennedy, who had always imagined a more perfect America. The press began referring to his term as "the Camelot White House."

THE KENNEDY FAMILY

Father Joseph Patrick Kennedy (1888–1969)

Occupation Financier, diplomat

Mother Rose Elizabeth Fitzgerald Kennedy (1890–1995)

Wife Jacqueline Lee Bouvier Kennedy

Birth July 28, 1929, Southampton, New York

The Kennedys vacationing in Hyannis Port with their dogs.

Marriage September 12, 1953

Occupation Newspaper reporter/photographer; book editor

Death May 19, 1994, New York, New York

Children Arabella (1956); Caroline Bouvier Kennedy (b. 1957); John Fitzgerald Kennedy Jr. (1960–1999); Patrick Bouvier Kennedy (1963)

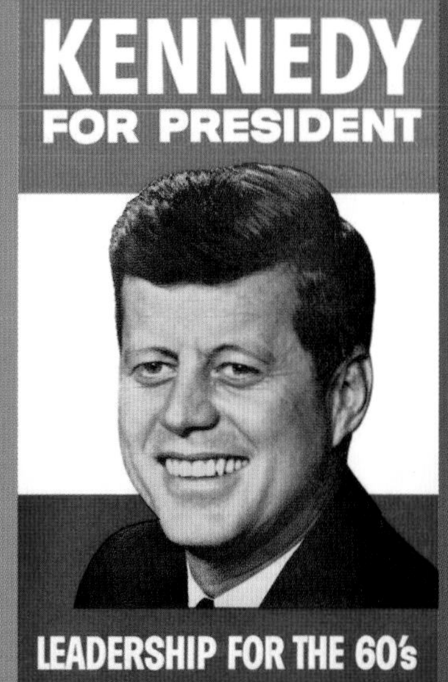

DID YOU KNOW . . . ?

- JFK was the only president of the Roman Catholic faith.
- He was the first Boy Scout to grow up to be president.
- He wrote his Pulitzer Prize–winning book, *Profiles in Courage*, while recovering from a serious back operation.
- JFK relied on a particular make of rocking chair to relieve his constant back pain. He had at least 14 made, including ones for the Oval Office and Air Force One.

A 1962 photo shows the first lady enjoying a horseback ride with John Jr. seated in front of her, while Caroline keeps up on her pony Macaroni.

JFK AND THE SPACE RACE

"Astro-chimp" Ham gives a handshake welcome to the recovery ship's commander after his flight. Ham was trained to test-fly space capsules.

Just over a month after cosmonaut Yuri Gagarin took the title of first human in space, orbiting the earth in the Soviet *Vostok* spacecraft on April 12, 1961, President Kennedy spoke before a joint session of Congress, issuing a challenge to land humans on the moon before the end of the decade. His goal? To make sure that the United States did not fall farther behind in the Cold War space race.

In 1961 NASA's Project Mercury sent a male chimpanzee, Ham, into space in a capsule designed for human astronauts. The same year, Alan Shepard became the first American in space aboard the Mercury-Redstone 3 capsule dubbed *Freedom 7*. In 1962 John Glenn made history as the first human to orbit earth aboard *Friendship 7*.

Kennedy did not live to see his ultimate goal fulfilled. Yet America did win the space race, when, on July 20, 1969, two Americans became the first humans to walk on the moon.

President Kennedy inspects the Mercury capsule *Friendship 7* with astronaut John Glenn.

> "A man may die, nations may rise and fall, but an idea lives on."
>
> —John F. Kennedy

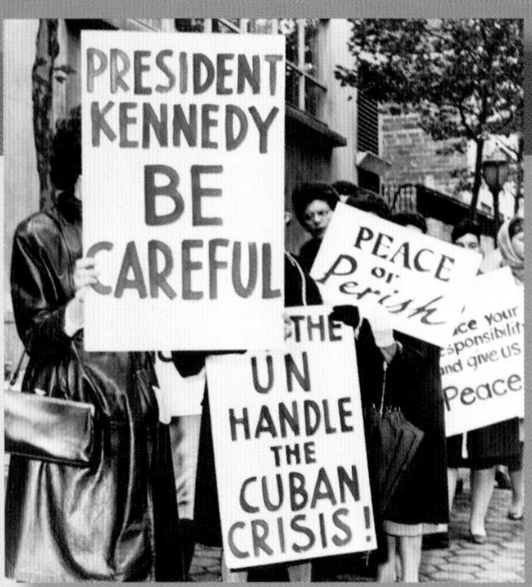

A crowd of 800 members of Women for Peace gathers near the United Nations building to protest during the Cuban Missile Crisis in 1962.

THE CUBAN MISSILE CRISIS

For two tense weeks in October 1962, the world held its breath as President Kennedy and Soviet premier Nikita Khrushchev squared off over the issue of Soviet missile bases in Cuba. After aerial surveillance photos showed missile installations being erected in Cuba, JFK appeared on television on October 22 to declare that "it shall be the policy of this nation to regard any nuclear missile launched from Cuba against any nation in the Western Hemisphere as an attack on the United States, requiring a full retaliatory response upon the Soviet Union." JFK ordered a naval blockade preventing any Soviet ships from reaching the island, and cautioned the American armed forces to stay on alert. The Soviets finally agreed to dismantle the bases in return for the removal of American bases in Turkey. JFK called the compromise "an important and constructive contribution to peace."

CAROLINE AND JOHN JR.

The Kennedy's two young children, Caroline and John Jr.—called "John-John" by the press—charmed America. John was born only weeks after the election, and so the public watched him grow up in the White House.

"The whole world knew his name before he did."

—Ted Kennedy, about John Jr.

John Jr. takes a stroll with his father at the White House in 1963. Inset: Before his death in a 1999 plane crash, John Jr. was a lawyer and publisher.

Top: Caroline with her father aboard the Kennedy yacht in 1963. Bottom: Caroline, the sole survivor of the family, at the John F. Kennedy Presidential Library and Museum in Boston. She is now a writer and a lawyer.

Caroline loved animals and was often photographed with her many pets, including Macaroni, her pony; Pushinka, the daughter of Strelka, a space dog that was a gift from Khrushchev; and even a flock of ducklings. John Jr. often accompanied Kennedy on walks along the beach at Hyannis Port, appearing to copy his father's thoughtful attitude. John-John's salute as his father's casket passed by on Pennsylvania Avenue touched the hearts of grieving Americans everywhere and came to symbolize the nation's loss.

FAMILY TRAGEDIES

Many people have observed that the Kennedy family suffered so many personal tragedies that it seemed almost to be cursed. This is not an extreme conclusion if you consider the death of Kennedy's older brother, Joseph, during World War II, the death of his sister Kathleen shortly after it, the assassinations of Kennedy and younger brother Robert, and the accidental death of John Jr., who died with his wife and sister-in-law while piloting a small plane.

The Kennedys in Hyannis Port, 1948. From left: John, Jean, Rose, Joseph Sr., Pat, Bobby, Eunice, and Ted. The two eldest siblings, Joe Jr. and Kathleen, had already died.

Timeline of the Kennedy Presidency

US Events / **World Events**

1960 (US) Etch-a-Sketch hits stores

1961 (World) The Beatles perform for the first time in Liverpool, England

1961 (US) Bob Dylan releases first album

1961 (World) The Soviets detonate a 58-megaton hydrogen bomb, creating the largest human-made explosion on record

1961 (US) A plane crash kills the entire US figure skating team

1962 (World) Jawaharlal Nehru is elected prime minister of India

1962 (US) Wilt Chamberlain scores 100 points in one basketball game for the Philadelphia Warriors

1962 (US) Rachel Carson's book *Silent Spring* is released, leading to the environmental movement

1962 (World) German war criminal Adolf Eichmann is hanged in Israel

1963 (US) Coca-Cola debuts its first diet soft drink, Tab cola

1963 (US) Civil rights leader Dr. Martin Luther King Jr. delivers his "I have a dream" speech

1963 (World) A volcanic eruption under the sea near Iceland creates a new island, Surtsey

Lyndon B. Johnson

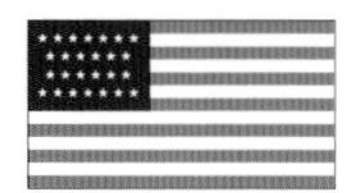

"LBJ"

1963–1969

Tall Texan Lyndon Johnson was a savvy and seasoned politician who kept the nation moving forward after the shock of Kennedy's death. He signed a groundbreaking civil rights act and created the Great Society, yet his term was troubled by the ongoing Vietnam War.

Johnson was a self-made man in the old log-cabin tradition. He was born to a poor family in Central Texas and worked hard to get an education. As a teacher he gained compassion for minorities after seeing the plight of the poverty-stricken Mexicans in his classroom—a lesson he carried straight to the White House.

With the aid of wife "Lady Bird" he successfully ran for Congress in 1937. During World War II his brief stint as a naval observer earned him a Silver Star. He served six terms in the House before he was elected to the Senate, where he became the youngest minority leader in its history. The following year a political shift to the Democrats made him majority leader.

Taking the Reins

The Democrats chose him to run with Kennedy, expecting him to pull in the valuable Southern vote. After Kennedy's assassination in 1963, Johnson became the second Texan in the White House after Eisenhower. He enacted the legislation Kennedy had been supporting—a civil rights bill and a tax cut—but also challenged Americans "to build a great society, a place where the meaning of man's life matches the marvels of man's labor."

Voters elected Johnson in his own right in 1964 by the widest margin in American history. He now had a mandate to make the Great Society a reality, and he urged legislation for improving education, combating crime, increasing urban housing, fighting disease, and established programs for Medicare, national beautification, and a "War on Poverty." With his encouragement NASA's conquest of space continued, and in 1968 three astronauts actually orbited the moon.

"The noblest search is the search for excellence."

Although Johnson actively supported civil rights with anti-discrimination policies, as president he had to seek solutions on the side of law and order. Meanwhile black unrest increased, and rioting broke out in the ghettos of many American cities

In spite of Johnson's attempts to peacefully end Communist aggression in South Vietnam, he was unable to negotiate a truce. The war, and Johnson's presidency, grew increasingly unpopular, with protesters rallying in the streets and marching on Washington, DC. Johnson chose not to run for a second term, insisting he wanted to devote all his energies to the quest for peace in Southeast Asia. The former president died of a heart attack in 1973 while peace talks were under way.

BIOGRAPHICAL FACTS

Birth August 27, 1908, near Johnson City, Texas

Religion Disciples of Christ

Education Southwest Texas State Teachers College (graduated 1930)

Occupation Teacher; rancher

Other Offices Congressional secretary; member of US House of Representatives; US senator; vice president

Military Service Lieutenant commander, US Navy

Political Party Democratic

Vice President Hubert H. Humphrey

Age at Inauguration 55

Death January 22, 1973, near Johnson City, Texas

The first lady gained her nickname from a nursemaid, who said she was "pretty as a lady bird."

Timeline of the Johnson Presidency

US Events / **World Events**

1964 (US) Word's Fair opens in Flushing Meadows, New York

1964 (US) Cassius Clay (Muhammad Ali) beats Sonny Liston for the heavyweight crown

1965 (World) Spirograph is introduced at the Nuremberg International Toy Fair.

1965 (US) G.I. Joe is introduced

1966 (World) Indira Gandhi is elected prime minister of India

1966 (US) Holiday classic *How the Grinch Stole Christmas* premiers on TV

1966 (US) The game Twister hits stores

1967 (World) Kenyan archaeologist Louis Leakey discovers pre-human fossils in Kenya

1967 (US) American theoretical physicist John Archibald Wheeler first uses the term "black hole"

1968 (US) Summer of Love in San Francisco; on the East Coast *Hair* debuts on Broadway

1968 (US) Civil rights leader Dr. Martin Luther King Jr. is assassinated

1968 (World) North Korea seizes USS *Pueblo* for "violating" their waters

DOGS, DOGS, DOGS

The Johnsons were avid pet-lovers, and their White House days included lots of dogs. Him and Her, the most famous of them, were beagles. Their daughter added Freckles to the family, while another beagle, J. Edgar, joined them after Him and Her died. Blanco, a white collie, came to live at the White House in 1963. The last of them, Yuki, gained a presidential home when Luci found him in a gas station on Thanksgiving Day 1966.

Shaking Blanco's paw.

Her and Him.

Singing with Yuki.

LBJ ALL THE WAY

"Every President wants to do right."

—Lyndon Johnson

THE JOHNSON FAMILY

Father Sam Ealy Johnson Jr. (1877–1937)

Occupation State representative; publisher; landowner

Mother Rebekah Baines Johnson (1881–1958)

Wife Claudia Alta "Lady Bird" Taylor Johnson

Birth December 22, 1912, Karnack, Texas

Marriage November 17, 1934

Death July 11, 2007, Austin, Texas

Children Lynda Bird (b. 1944); Luci Baines (b. 1947)

The Johnson family shortly before moving into the White House. From left: Lynda, Luci, LBJ, and Lady Bird. Both daughters were married during LBJ's term. Lynda's wedding was held in the East Room.

The First Lady

Lady Bird Johnson, Pat Nixon, Nancy Reagan, Barbara Bush, Rosalynn Carter, and Betty Ford.

The woman who acts as White House hostess usually takes the title "first lady." Most often she is the wife of the president, but in the past an unmarried or widowed president relied on a daughter, sister, niece, or even a family friend to serve as hostess. For example, Dolley Madison acted as first lady (though the title was not in use yet) for the widowed Thomas Jefferson as well as for her husband, James. The first lady has often been the president's confidante, advisor, campaign assistant, and his source of strength.

In the late 19th century, women took on more responsibilities outside the home, and first ladies also took on larger roles, often supporting various causes. The modern first lady's duties may include attending state functions, greeting dignitaries, holding press conferences, meeting with schoolchildren or residents of nursing homes, and generally serving as the president's goodwill ambassador. She often supports charities and other humanitarian organizations or takes on a specific cause, such as literacy or ending hunger. Some first ladies have also had young children of their own to look after in addition to their public responsibilities.

"Any lady who is first lady likes being first lady. I don't care what they say, they like it."

—Richard M. Nixon

First Ladies Speak Out

Martha Washington

"I live a very dull life here . . . indeed I think I am more like a state prisoner than anything else."

Julia Gardiner Tyler

"Nothing appears to delight the President more than . . . to hear people sing my praises."

Julia Grant

"My life at the White House was like a bright and beautiful dream . . . quite the happiest period of my life."

Edith Roosevelt

"Being in the center of things is very interesting, yet the same proportions remain. . . . I don't believe I have been forced into the 'first lady of the land' model of my predecessors."

ORIGIN OF THE TITLE

Dolley Madison

During America's formative years, there was no formal title for the president's wife or hostess. Martha Washington preferred "Lady Washington," and such titles as "Mrs. President" and even "Mrs. Presidentress" were later used. In a eulogy for Dolley Madison, Zachary Taylor may have called her the "first lady," but there's no record of his exact wording. The title was in use in Washington, DC, around 1850 and gained national awareness in 1877 when journalist Mary C. Ames described Lucy Webb Hayes as "the first lady of the land" while reporting on the Hayes inauguration. Mrs. Hayes became very popular, and newspaper coverage of her activities helped spread the use of the term.

The National First Ladies' Library, which features biographies, photos, and oral histories, is housed in the Canton, Ohio, home of First Lady Ida McKinley.

"Being first lady is the hardest unpaid job in the world."

—Pat Nixon

The US Mint currently honors first spouses by issuing collectible gold coins in their images. Left is the Martha Washington coin.

> "A first lady is in a position to know the needs of the country and do something about them. It would be a shame not to take full advantage of that power."
>
> —Rosalynn Carter

FACING ADVERSITY

The world watched as Jacqueline Kennedy mourned her husband.

Who could ever forget the sight of Jacqueline Kennedy standing stricken beside Lyndon Johnson as he was sworn in immediately after the assassination of John Kennedy? Yet Jacqueline showed herself to be a woman of dignity and courage during the aftermath. Many first wives have had to share their mourning for a departed husband with the whole nation. While some withdrew from the public eye, others put aside their grief and took their places in the funeral corteges, providing examples of grace during adversity and proving that great men often marry remarkable women.

First Ladies Speak Out

Helen Herron Taft
"I had always had the satisfaction of knowing almost as much as he about the politics and intricacies of any situation in which he found himself, and my life was filled with interests of a most unusual kind."

Florence Harding
"Well, Warren Harding, I have got you the presidency. What are you going to do with it?"

Lou Henry Hoover
"I majored in geology in college but have majored in Herbert Hoover ever since."

Eleanor Roosevelt
"I could not at any age be content to take my place in a corner by the fireside and simply look on."

Mamie Eisenhower
"Ike runs the country and I turn the pork chops."

Jacqueline Kennedy
"The one thing I do not want to be called is First Lady. It sounds like a saddle horse."

Betty Ford
"[It's] not my power, but the power of the position, a power which could be used to help."

Nancy Reagan
"I see the first lady as another means to keep a president from becoming isolated."

Hillary Clinton
"Probably my worst quality is that I get very passionate about what I think is right."

Laura Bush
"I'm not the one who was elected. I would never do anything to undermine my husband's point of view."

FIRST LADY FACTS

- She dressed fashionably in public, but at home Martha Washington often wore housedresses remade from curtains.
- The well-educated Sarah Polk was the first first lady to attend cabinet meetings.
- Margaret Taylor became the first widow in the White House.
- Abigail Fillmore, a former schoolteacher, established the first official library in the Executive Mansion.
- Florence Harding was first first lady to vote.
- Grace Coolidge taught deaf children.
- Hillary Clinton was the first first lady to have earned a law degree.
- Laura Bush was the only first lady to have given birth to twins.

Grace Coolidge with her dog Rob Roy. The first lady was once a teacher to the deaf.

Richard M. Nixon

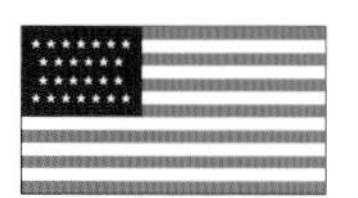

"Tricky Dick"

1969–1974

When he entered the White House, Richard Nixon was already an experienced legislator with a reputation as an anti-Communist leader. But his ambition outweighed his caution, and after the Watergate investigation linked him to illegal activities, he resigned from office.

"A man is not finished when he is defeated. He is finished when he quits."

Nixon was born in Southern California, to Quaker parents. He proved himself a brilliant student a Whittier College and then at Duke University Law School. After his marriage to Pat Ryan, whom he met in a local theater group, Nixon began to practice law. He served in the Pacific during World War II and was elected to Congress on his return. He gained a seat in the Senate in 1950, and the Republicans tapped him to run with Eisenhower in 1952. When his use of campaign "slush funds" was questioned, he defended himself on TV with the famous "Checkers" speech, detailing his complete financial history but refusing to return one of the campaign gifts: his daughters' pet cocker spaniel.

As vice president, Nixon oversaw the government three times when Eisenhower was ill. His own bid for president in 1960 failed, partly because Kennedy claimed the Eisenhower-Nixon team had not kept up with Soviet military technology.

Making a Comeback

Nixon lost a bid for governor of California in 1962, and it seemed his career in politics was over. Yet he rallied and beat Vice President Hubert Humphrey in the 1968 presidential election, crediting America's "silent majority"—voters who wanted a return to conservatism. Nixon used his skills as a negotiator to improve relations with the USSR and China and then set about ending the unpopular Vietnam War. Meanwhile, he ordered secret bombings of Communist targets in Cambodia and Laos. In 1970, when the National Guard killed four student war protesters at Kent State in Ohio, Nixon's apparent lack of sympathy sparked a nationwide student strike. Nixon won reelection in 1972 by a landslide. When the press revealed that several men had broken into Democratic Party headquarters at the Watergate Hotel in Washington, Nixon attempted to cover up his involvement. But other "dirty tricks" soon came to light, including illegal wiretapping and plans to discredit members of the press. Nixon went on TV to declare, "I am not a crook," but in spite of his claims the House Judiciary Committee opened impeachment hearings. Nixon resigned on August 4, 1974. President Gerald Ford formally pardoned him the same year.

Later successes in foreign affairs helped Nixon rebuild his image, and when he died in 1994, some observers even regarded him as an "elder statesman."

BIOGRAPHICAL FACTS

Birth January 9, 1913, Yorba Linda, California

Religion Quaker

Education Whittier College (graduated 1934); Duke University Law School (graduated 1937)

Occupation Lawyer

Other Offices Attorney for US Office of Emergency Management; member of US House of Representatives; US senator; vice president

Military Service Lieutenant commander, Naval Reserve

Political Party Republican

Vice President Spiro T. Agnew; Gerald R. Ford

Age at Inauguration 56

Death April 22, 1994, New York, New York

Although the press was hard on Pat Nixon, she was very popular with the public.

DID YOU KNOW. . . ?

- Nixon's great-grandfather George Nixon III died at the Battle of Gettysburg.
- Nixon took the oath of office on two Bibles: the Ryan and the Nixon family Bibles, held by Pat.
- Nixon was the first US president to visit all 50 states, as well as the first to visit the Soviet Union.

Wearing a proud smile, the president escorts his daughter Tricia down the aisle to meet her groom, Edward Cox. The lavish 1971 White House wedding featured a Rose Garden ceremony. Nixon's younger daughter, Julie, was also married after her father was elected president but before his inauguration.

Pasha, Vicky, and King Timahoe, the Nixon dogs.

"I brought myself down. I impeached myself by resigning."

—Richard M. Nixon

Protesters call for Nixon's impeachment during a White House demonstration.

THE NIXON FAMILY

Father Francis Anthony Nixon (1878–1956)

Occupation Gas station and general store owner

Mother Hannah Milhous Nixon (1885–1967)

Wife Thelma "Pat" Catherine Ryan Nixon

Birth March 16, 1912, Ely, Nevada

Marriage June 21, 1940

Death June 22, 1993, Park Ridge, New Jersey

Children Patricia (b. 1946); Julie (b. 1948)

Nixon's farewell.

Timeline of the Nixon Presidency

US Events | **World Events**

1969 (World) Yasser Arafat is appointed leader of the Palestine Liberation Organization (PLO)

1969 (US) Astronaut Neil Armstrong becomes the first human to walk on the moon

1969 Woodstock Music and Art Fair held in Bethel, New York

1970 (World) Aswan High Dam in Egypt is completed

1970 (US) The first Earth Day

1970 (US) Oxygen tank explosion forces end of *Apollo 13* mission

1970 (World) Isle of Wight Festival becomes largest rock concert with 600,000 in attendance

1971 (US) Amtrak begins intercity passenger rail service

1971 (World) Bangladesh is created from a former Pakistan territory

1972 (US) Magnavox introduces Odyssey, the first video game machine

1972 (World) British physicist Stephen Hawking confined to wheelchair due to motor neuron disease

1973 (US) Dave Arneson and Scott Gygax invent Dungeons & Dragons

Gerald R. Ford

"Boy Scout in the White House"

1974–1977

As the first president to take the oath after a predecessor's resignation, Gerald Ford faced the task of restoring the faith of a country that had come to mistrust the highest office in the land.

Ford was born in Nebraska and grew up in Grand Rapids, Michigan. A talented athlete, he was a football hero at the University of Michigan and coached football at Yale while completing his law degree. During World War II he served in the navy as a lieutenant commander aboard the aircraft carrier *Monterey*. He always believed his experiences abroad had turned him into an "internationalist." Ford returned to Grand Rapids to practice law and entered the House of Representatives in 1948, the same year he wed Betty Bloomer Warren.

During his 25-year tenure in Congress, Ford became known for his honesty and open manner. He was Nixon's choice in 1973 to replace departing vice president Spiro Agnew, who was under investigation for tax evasion. The following year Nixon himself resigned and Ford was now president—without having been elected to either office.

A Time for Healing

One of Ford's first acts was to pardon Nixon, hoping it would heal the traumatized country. This proved a controversial decision, and its unpopularity might have damaged Ford's run for president in 1976. He also offered conditional amnesty to Vietnam "draft dodgers"—men who left the United States rather than fight a war that they opposed.

On the domestic front, Ford battled to curb rising inflation, revive a flagging economy, and solve the ongoing energy crisis. He also reduced corporate taxes and eased regulations on business, hoping to stimulate the economy. Faced with a Democratic Congress after the post-Watergate elections, Ford frequently used the presidential veto, but Congress overrode him more times than any president since Andrew Johnson in the 1860s.

"Truth is the glue that holds government together."

Ford knew he had to preserve America's status in the world, especially after Vietnam and Cambodia fell to the Communists. In 1975, to avert the threat of war in the Middle East, the Ford administration was able to negotiate an interim truce agreement between Egypt and Israel, partly by agreeing to give aid to both nations. Ford also signed an agreement with Soviet leader Leonid Brezhnev to limit nuclear weapons. In 1975 he—along with the leaders of the Soviet Union and 33 other nations—signed the Declaration of Helsinki, which required the Soviet Union to respect human rights.

Ford ran for president in 1976 but lost to Jimmy Carter, who later became a close friend. He remained in the public eye, however, often attending state ceremonies. He was 93 when he died at his California home. His son Michael, an Evangelical minister, performed the last rites.

BIOGRAPHICAL FACTS

Birth July 14, 1913, Omaha, Nebraska

Religion Episcopalian

Education University of Michigan (graduated 1935); Yale University Law School (graduated 1941)

Occupation Lawyer

Other Offices Member of US House of Representatives; vice president

Military Service Lieutenant commander, US Navy

Ford playing football at the University of Michigan.

Political Party Republican

Vice President Nelson Rockefeller

Age at Inauguration 61

Death December 26, 2006, Rancho Mirage, California

The Fords with first dog Liberty. After suffering from chemical dependency herself, the former first lady founded the Betty Ford Center to help others battle drug and alcohol addiction.

Above: The Fords, with daughter Susan, show off the newest additions to the first family: Liberty's newborn puppies.

Left: Susan with Chan the cat.

DID YOU KNOW. . . ?

- Ford's birth name was Leslie Lynch King Jr. His parents separated when he was only two weeks old. He took his stepfather's name at age two, when his mother remarried.
- As a youth Ford achieved the rank of Eagle Scout.
- Ford was the longest-lived US president to date.
- First pets were Liberty, a golden retriever, and Chan, a Siamese cat. Liberty gave birth to a litter of puppies while at the White House.

THE FORD FAMILY

Stepfather Gerald Rudolph Ford (1890–1962)

Occupation President of Ford Paint and Varnish

Mother Dorothy Ayer Gardner King Ford (1892–1967)

Wife Elizabeth "Betty" Ann Bloomer Warren Ford

Birth April 8, 1918, Chicago, Illinois

Marriage October 15, 1948

The Fords at the White House: Mike; his wife, Gayle; the president; the first lady; Jack; Susan; and Steve.

Children Michael Gerald (b. 1950); John Gardner (b. 1952); Steven Meigs (b. 1956); Susan (b. 1957)

Timeline of the Ford Presidency

US Events | **World Events**

1974 (US) *People* magazine first hits newstandss

1974 (World) World population reaches four billion

1974 (US) Ronald DeFeo Jr. murders his parents and siblings in the Amityville "Horror House" in Long Island, New York

1974 (World) A significant "upright walking" skeleton from the hominid species *Australopithecus afarensis* is discovered in Ethiopia and named Lucy

1975 (US) John N. Mitchell, H. R. Haldeman, and John Ehrlichman are found guilty of the Watergate coverup

1975 (World) The UN proclaims March 8 International Women's Day

1975 (US) TV's *Wheel of Fortune* premiers

1976 (US) America celebrates its bicentennial on the 200th anniversary of the signing of the Declaration of Independence

1976 (World) First known outbreak of ebola virus in Yambuku, Zaire

1976 (US) Gambling casinos legalized in Atlantic City, New Jersey

1976 (US) Nolan Bushnell sells his video game company, Atari, to Warner Brothers

Jimmy Carter

"The Man from Plains" **1977–1981**

39th President

Behind James Earl "Jimmy" Carter's homespun manner and relaxed drawl lay a sharp mind and deep humanitarian values. Economic problems at home and spreading unrest abroad, however, undermined his presidency.

Carter was born in the small town of Plains, Georgia. After attending the US Naval Academy, he planned to make a career in the Navy and served in the new nuclear submarine program. When his father died seven years later, however, Carter returned home to run the family business. He was elected to the Georgia State Senate in 1962 and rose to governor of the state eight years later.

His bid for the presidency in 1975 at first gained little momentum, but his lack of Washington connections eventually proved a benefit: in the cautious post-Nixon climate he seemed untainted by questionable political alliances. He beat Gerald Ford in a close election and became the first president from the Deep South since 1848.

As he had done as governor, Carter favored progressive legislation, supporting integration and environmental protection and offering unconditional amnesty to draft dodgers. He increased employment by eight million jobs and placed a record number of minorities and women in federal jobs. His administration saw the creation of two cabinet-level departments: the Department of Energy and the Department of Education.

"It's not necessary to fear the prospect of failure but to be determined not to fail."

In addition to opening full diplomatic relations with China, Carter established a peace treaty between Egypt and Israel with the Camp David Accords. He focused on human rights issues in the Soviet Union rather than on military rivalry.

Trouble Arises

As the national fuel shortage worsened and lines at the gas pump increased, the Congress that had at first supported Carter began to oppose him. The Soviet Union's invasion of Afghanistan put a halt to American arms negotiations with the Russians, and when Iranian student extremists took over the US embassy and took 52 Americans hostage, the country seemed to turn on Carter. For 14 months he worked for the release of the hostages, but it was not until the day he left office that they were freed. New president Ronald Reagan sent Carter to greet them in Europe.

As a private citizen, former president Carter wrote 27 books, founded an institute to promote global health and human rights, and remains an activist for Habitat for Humanity, which builds affordable housing. In 2002 the peanut farmer from Plains was awarded the Nobel Peace Prize.

BIOGRAPHICAL FACTS

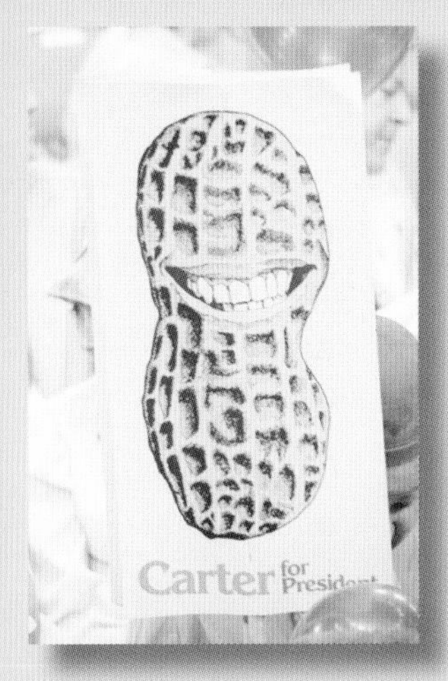

Birth October 1, 1924, Plains, Georgia

Religion Baptist

Education United States Naval Academy (graduated 1946)

Occupation Peanut farmer; author; nuclear engineer

His former career and his wide smile inspired the "Carter for President" sign showing a peanut shell with a toothy grin.

Other Offices Georgia state senator; governor of Georgia

Military Service Lieutenant commander, US Navy

Political Party Democratic

Vice President Walter Mondale

Age at Inauguration 52

DID YOU KNOW . . . ?

Even in his eighties, the former president continues working on humanitarian projects, such as building houses for Habitat for Humanity.

- Carter can speed read; he's been recorded reading 2,000 words per minute.
- Carter was the first president to send his mother on a diplomatic mission.
- His favorite foods are mixed nuts and peaches.
- The Carters volunteer with Habitat for Humanity, a program that helps low-income workers to build and purchase their own homes.

The former president recognizes Rosalynn Carter's contribution to his success, crediting her as a "full partner." As first lady, Rosalynn was known for her mental health reform efforts. She continues this work today.

THE CARTER FAMILY

Father James Earl Carter (1894–1953)

Occupation Grocer

Mother Bessie Lillian Gordy Carter (1898–1983)

Occupation Nurse

Wife Eleanor Rosalynn Smith Carter

Birth August 18, 1927, Plains, Georgia

Marriage July 7, 1946

Occupation Dressmaker; peanut farmer; public health advocate

Amy Carter with her Siamese cat, Misty Malarky Ying-Yang.

Children John "Jack" (b. 1947); James Earl III "Chip" (b. 1950); Donnel Jeffrey "Jeff" (b. 1952); Amy Lynn (b. 1967)

Timeline of the Carter Presidency

US Events / **World Events**

1977 (World) Queen Elizabeth II commences her Silver Jubilee

1977 (US) David Berkowitz, the Son of Sam serial killer, is captured in Yonkers, New York

1978 (World) In the United Kingdom, Louise Brown becomes the first human born from in vitro fertilization

1978 (US) Volkswagen becomes the first foreign auto manufacturer to open a US plant

1978 (World) John Paul II becomes the first Polish pope in history

1979 (US) A major gay rights march takes place in Washington, DC

1979 (World) Islamic fundamentalist Ayatollah Ruhollah Khomeini seizes power in Iran

1979 (World) The first black-led government in 90 years takes control of Rhodesia

1980 (US) Mount St. Helens in Washington State erupts, killing 57

1980 (US) A fan kills former Beatle John Lennon in New York City

1980 (World) Spring Rhythms, the first rock music festival in the Soviet Union, takes place in Georgia

Presidents in a Global Economy

In 2007 former presidents George H. W. Bush, Jimmy Carter, and Bill Clinton gathered together at the dedication of the Billy Graham Library. The presidents of the late 20th century faced the challenges that came with a world that, through technology, seemed to have shrunk to a "global village."

The last decade of the 20th century brought new challenges to the United States and its leaders. The Cold War was all but over, and the nation was establishing trade relations with former enemies, but threats to national security and individual welfare still loomed.

"No generation has had the opportunity, as we now have, to build a global economy that leaves no one behind. It is a wonderful opportunity, but also a profound responsibility."

—Bill Clinton

The Middle East, the countries between the Mediterranean Sea and the Persian Gulf, were in turmoil. Arab nations continued to harass Israel, and Israel responded with military force. Centuries-old feuds provoked Arab countries to war with one another in this oil-rich but strife-ridden area. US industry required foreign oil, and so the country entered into these conflicts, trying to reestablish peace but also arousing the hatred of extremists who felt that the US military had no right to cross their borders.

One kind of warfare arose in greater scale than ever before—terrorism. Terrorists often had no national allegiance; they were unified by a set of beliefs rather than by patriotism. They traveled from country to country, setting off bombs, assassinating leaders, and creating chaos. They operated below government radar in secret groups called cells. Identifying their locations was nearly impossible, even with interrogation, because one cell rarely knew the members of another cell.

Another serious threat to America came in the form of a microscopic retrovirus called HIV, or human immunodeficiency virus, which led to a potentially fatal disease called AIDS, or acquired immunodeficiency syndrome. Researchers came up with treatments to control this deadly medical time bomb but have yet to find a cure.

The carbon emissions from millions of cars and factories began to deteriorate the atmosphere, causing a climate change called global warming. As more solar heat penetrated the atmosphere, polar ice began to melt and the air and water currents that regulate global temperatures began to alter. Alarmed scientists campaigned for restrictions on emissions, and American leaders, who were at first skeptical, finally began to heed them.

A Global Voice

At the end of the last century, a revolutionary new form of communication sprang up: the Internet, or World Wide Web. This electronic network allows people all over the world to communicate through their personal computers, creating what some have called a "global village." Businesspeople now conduct international deals and transfer funds without ever leaving the office. The government has to oversee not only commerce in the immediate country but also business transactions worldwide.

The United States has always understood that not only a strong military but also a thriving economy determined its stature in the world. But now the question became, how much global economy was good for America?

The benefits of operating abroad were clear: cheaper labor and fewer restrictions. But American workers protested the loss of jobs to overseas workers. Many smaller cities that relied on single industries watched with dismay as their means of support relocated to foreign lands, leaving them virtual ghost towns.

The nation's leaders also had to deal with the rise of the "mega-corporation." Mergers and acquisitions between companies created huge corporations that often controlled what had once been separate industries, such as publishing and entertainment. With the power of money and the influence it buys behind them, these mega-corporations form a mighty lobby, capable of swaying US leaders. Pharmaceutical giants have used their clout to influence legislation. The United States has fought several wars in the Middle East, in part to ensure the flow of petroleum products to powerful oil companies.

As the nation moves forward into the new millennium, future presidents will not only be faced with keeping a balance of military power, but also with regulating trade and preventing the mega-corporations from dominating the commercial, and political, landscape.

WHAT DOES THAT MEAN?

Extremists People who go to great or exaggerated lengths to achieve a goal

Lobby A group representing a specific interest that seeks to influence lawmakers in its favor

Mega-corporations Huge corporations formed by the merger of several, often diverse companies that then operate under the same "brand" umbrella

COLLIDING SPHERES

On the morning of September 11, 2001, foreign terrorists hijacked four American Airlines jets. One of the planes slammed into the Pentagon in Washington, and a second crashed down into a Pennsylvania field before reaching its undisclosed target. But it is significant that two of the planes flew into the twin towers of the World Trade Center in New York City, resulting in their destruction. The World Trade Center was not a military installation but a center of commerce and home to many financial firms. It seemed that the spheres of politics and business had become entwined as targets in the eyes of those who wished the nation harm. It was clear that these extremists not only viewed America's military might as a threat, but its culture and economy as well.

Ronald Reagan

"The Gipper"

1981–1989

Ronald Reagan, a former movie actor, was a powerful president whose skill at negotiating with both Congress and foreign leaders resulted in a strengthening of the national economy and the easing of tensions abroad.

Reagan was born above a bank in Tampico, Illinois, and as a youth excelled at athletics. He took a job as a radio sports announcer after graduating from Eureka College, and in 1937 a Hollywood screen test led to a career as an actor. With his "boy next door" good looks, he soon became a leading man.

While president of the Screen Actors Guild, Reagan testified on the influence of communism in the entertainment industry and afterward made the switch from liberal to conservative politics.

After two terms as governor of California, he was nominated for president in 1980 with Texan George H. W. Bush as his running mate. Considering the Carter administration's problems with the economy and foreign terrorists, it wasn't surprising that the Republicans were swept into office. The day Reagan took office, the 52 US hostages in Iran finally received their freedom.

A President to Be Reckoned With

Reagan immediately took control of Congress, which allowed him to stimulate the sluggish economy and curb inflation by instituting major tax cuts, slowing nondefense spending and removing many regulations on business. He also believed in "peace through strength" and increased the military budget by 40 percent. His system of "Reaganomics" had positive results, but it also greatly increased both the deficit and the national debt.

Two months after Reagan took office, he was shot by John Hinckley Jr. but quickly recovered.

The Reagan-Bush ticket won again in 1984 by the largest margin of electoral votes in history. Reagan, who had once called the Soviets "the evil empire," now sought a diplomatic path to peace. He negotiated arms agreements four times with Soviet leader Mikhail Gorbachev, and they eventually signed a treaty eliminating midrange nuclear weapons. In 1989, just months after Reagan left office, the Berlin Wall came down, and the Soviet Union collapsed. The Cold War had ended.

"Mr. Gorbachev, tear down this wall!"

Reagan's second term weathered several scandals, including the Iran-Contra Affair, which involved the secret sale of arms to US foe Iran in order to illegally fund right-wing rebels in Nicaragua. Reagan took full responsibility and suffered no formal repercussions. In 1994 he announced by letter that he suffered from Alzheimer's disease. Ten years later he died at his Bel-Air home. He is now viewed as a Republican icon, and his approval rating remains one of the highest of all presidents.

BIOGRAPHICAL FACTS

Reagan worked as a WHO radio announcer in Des Moines, Iowa, during the mid-1930s.

Birth February 6, 1911, Tampico, Illinois

Religion Episcopalian

Education Eureka College (graduated 1932)

Occupation Broadcaster; film actor

Other Offices Governor of California

Military Service Captain, US Army

Political Party Republican

Vice President George H. W. Bush

Age at Inauguration 69

Death June 5, 2004, Bel-Air, California

Nancy Reagan with the Reagans' lively King Charles spaniel, Rex, a press favorite. The first lady's "Just Say No" campaign against drug use received wide publicity.

DID YOU KNOW...?

- The famous phrase "Win one for the Gipper" came from Reagan's film *Knute Rockne, All American*. He had the role of George "The Gipper" Gipp, and the nickname stuck for life.
- As a lifeguard on the Rock River, Reagan said he saved 77 lives. He kept count by notching each rescue on a log.

Reagan as a lifeguard, 1927.

THE REAGAN FAMILY

Father John Edward Reagan (1883–1941)

Occupation Shoe salesman

Mother Nelle Clyde Wilson Reagan (1885–1962)

First Wife Jane Wyman Reagan (1914–2007)

Occupation Actress

Marriage January 26, 1940

Children Maureen (b. 1941); Michael (adopted) (b. 1945)

Second Wife Nancy Davis Reagan (b. 1921)

Occupation Actress

Marriage March 4, 1952

Children Patricia Ann (b. 1952); Ronald (b. 1958)

The Reagan family in 1976. From left to right: Patti, who took her mother's surname "Davis," Nancy; the president; Michael; Maureen; Ron; and dog Pogo.

Timeline of the Reagan Presidency

US Events | **World Events**

1981 (World) Turkish gunman shoots, and nearly kills, Pope John Paul II

1981 (World) Charles, Prince of Wales, marries Lady Diana Spencer

1982 (US) *Time* magazine's Man of the Year is the computer

1982 (World) The Falklands War begins between Britain and Argentina

1983 (US) Vanessa Williams crowned first African American Miss America

1984 (US) Apple's Macintosh goes on sale

1984 (World) Indian prime minister Indira Gandhi is assassinated

1985 (US) Microsoft releases Windows 1.0

1986 (US) Space shuttle *Challenger* disaster kills all onboard

1986 (World) The Chernobyl nuclear plant in the Ukraine explodes; it is the world's worst nuclear disaster

1986 (US) Xavier Roberts introduces Cabbage Patch Kids

1987 (World) World population reaches five billion

1988 (World) Terrorists blow up Pan Am Flight 103 over Lockerbie, Scotland, killing 270

George H. W. Bush

"The Last Cold Warrior"

1989–1993

With his signature phrase, "a kinder, gentler nation," George Bush brought traditional values to the White House, insisting that America could be a force for good.

Born in Massachusetts to a family with a history of public service, Bush grew up in Greenwich, Connecticut. In 1942 he enlisted in the navy at age 18 and became their youngest pilot—eventually flying 58 combat missions in the Pacific during World War II. In 1946 he married Barbara Pierce and enrolled at Yale to complete his education.

After embarking on a successful career in the Texas oil industry, Bush turned to politics. He served two terms in Congress representing Texas, followed by a series of high-level appointments: US ambassador to the UN, envoy to China, and director of the Central Intelligence Agency.

As Reagan's running mate in 1980, Bush helped bring in the critical Southern vote, and he was Reagan's natural successor eight years later.

After defeating Massachusetts Democrat Michael Dukakis, Bush entered the White House. At the time, the country was still benefiting from "Reaganomics," but the world beyond US borders was rapidly changing. The Soviet Union had dissolved into individual nations, and Soviet reformer Mikhail Gorbachev had resigned his office. Bush was now faced with new turmoil in Eastern Europe, and he chose to take a "wait and see" attitude. He did send US troops to Panama in 1989 to oust leader Manuel Noriega, who was suspected of spying for Cuba's Fidel Castro and of trafficking drugs to the United States.

War in the Desert

Another serious problem arose in the Middle East when Iraq, under dictator Saddam Hussein, invaded oil-rich Kuwait and then threatened American ally Saudi Arabia. Bush drew on the influence of the United Nations and rallied an international army to free Kuwait in an action known as Operation Desert Storm.

"We are a nation of communities . . . a brilliant diversity spread like stars, like a thousand points of light ."

Meanwhile, the US economy had begun to falter and the federal deficit continued to soar. Bush's campaign promise of "no new taxes" was not one he could stick to in that climate. Violent unrest in the nation's inner cities was also on the rise. Bush's initial popularity as the victor of Desert Storm could not withstand the fallout from these problems at home, and he lost the 1992 election to Democrat Bill Clinton.

Bush and Clinton later put party differences aside and became friends, working together to raise funds for victims of the 2004 Indian Ocean tsunami and Hurricane Katrina.

BIOGRAPHICAL FACTS

Birth June 12, 1924, Milton, Massachusetts

Religion Episcopalian

Education Yale University (graduated 1948)

Occupation Oil industry

Other Offices Member of US House of representatives; US ambassador to UN; US liaison to China; director of CIA; vice president

Military Service Lieutenant, US Navy

Political Party Republican

Vice President J. Danforth "Dan" Quayle

Age at Inauguration 64

Bush in an Avenger cockpit during his stint as a navy pilot.

Millie

MILLIE'S BOOK

Of all the famous White House pets, only one was ever credited as the "author" of a best-selling book. When Millie, the Bush's pet springer spaniel, gave birth to a litter of six puppies, the first lady wrote a book, calling it *Millie's Book: As Dictated to Barbara Bush.* Two of those pups also became presidential pets: the president took Ranger as his own, and the eldest Bush son took Spot. When George W. moved into the White House after his own election as president, Spot moved back in with him.

The first lady with Millie and Ranger, all in matching gray sweat suits.

Barbara Bush, with Millie. She was the second woman, after Abigail Adams, to be both wife and mother to a US president.

> "I'm conservative, but I'm not a nut about it."
>
> —George H. W. Bush

THE BUSH FAMILY

The Bush family in 1966. From left: Doro, George H., Jeb, Marvin, George W., Neil, and Barbara.

Father Prescott Bush (1895–1972)

Occupation Shoe salesman; US senator

Mother Dorothy Walker Bush (1901–1992)

Wife Barbara Pierce Bush

Birth June 8, 1925, Bronx, New York

Marriage January 6, 1945

Children George Walker (b. 1946); Robin (1949–1953); John Ellis "Jeb" (b. 1953); Neil (b. 1955); Marvin (b. 1956); Dorothy (b. 1959)

Timeline of the Bush Presidency

US Events / **World Events**

1989 (US) Nintendo introduces Gameboy, the first battery-powered, handheld video game system

1989 (World) Berlin Wall falls

1989 (US) *Exxon Valdez* spills millions of gallons of oil on coastline

1989 (World) Students massacred in China's Tiananmen Square

1990 (US) Hubble Telescope launched into space

1990 (World) Lech Walesa becomes president of Poland

1990 (World) South Africa's Nelson Mandela freed

1991 (World) Bronze Age man found frozen in glacier

1991 (World) Collapse of the Soviet Union

1991 (US) Operation Desert Storm

1991 (World) South Africa repeals apartheid laws

1992 (World) Official end of the Cold War

1992 (US) Minnesota's Mall of America, the largest shopping mall in the US, opens on 78 acres with an indoor amusement park

William J. Clinton

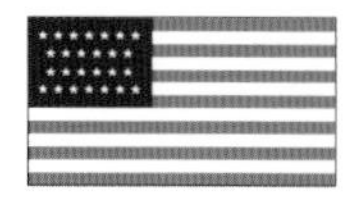

"The Man from Hope" **1993–2001**

During William J. Clinton's presidency the United States experienced a long stretch of prosperity, including record levels of employment, low inflation, and an actual budget surplus.

Clinton, named William Jefferson Blythe IV at birth, grew up in a small Arkansas town. "Bill" was an excellent student who loved reading. While in high school he was a delegate for Boy's Nation and met John F. Kennedy at the White House, a fateful encounter that whet his interest in politics.

After graduating from Georgetown, Clinton received a coveted Rhodes scholarship to Oxford University. He took his law degree from Yale in 1973 and two years later married Hillary Rodham, herself a graduate of Yale Law School. Clinton became Arkansas attorney general in 1976 and then governor in 1978—at 32 he was the youngest governor in the country. He lost a reelection bid but regained the office four years later. He served as governor until his successful run for the presidency in 1992, when he defeated incumbent George Bush by focusing on the flagging economy.

Triumphs and Tribulations

Clinton, like JFK, brought a youthful energy to the White House. He especially enjoyed jogging through the capital with his Secret Service escort in tow.

Two Clinton campaign promises, to allow openly gay people into the military and to reform the health care system, proved early stumbling blocks, but Clinton quickly recovered. He signed the Family Leave and Medical Act, the controversial North American Free Trade Agreement, and the Brady Bill, which required a waiting period for handgun purchases.

"We cannot build our own future without helping others to build theirs."

In 1996 Clinton became the first Democratic president since Franklin Roosevelt to gain a second term. In 1998 he ordered a four-day bombing of Iraq after Saddam Hussein obstructed United Nations weapons inspectors from completing their mission. When the "ethnic cleansing" of Albanians by Serbians in the former Yugoslavia began, Clinton sent in US troops to support a NATO action in Yugoslavia. He was less successful at resolving the Israeli-Palestinian conflict: both Middle Eastern leaders left the Camp David negotiations without reaching an accord.

In 1998 Clinton's indiscretions with a White House intern led to impeachment when he was accused of committing perjury (lying under oath) and of obstructing justice. The Senate acquitted him on both charges, but the trial increased the growing polarity between Republicans and Democrats.

After Clinton left office he worked for humanitarian causes and became a popular public speaker and author. He was active in wife Hillary's campaign for president in 2008.

BIOGRAPHICAL FACTS

Birth August 19, 1946, Hope, Arkansas
Religion Baptist
Education Georgetown University (graduated 1968); Oxford University (Rhodes Scholar); Yale University Law School (J.D., 1973)
Occupation Public speaker; law professor
Other Offices Attorney general of Arkansas; governor of Arkansas
Political Party Democratic
Vice President Albert Gore Jr.
Age at Inauguration 46

Clinton was a talented saxophone player and considered becoming a musician.

Hillary Clinton went from Bill's first lady to a political force in her own right.

> **"If I want to knock a story off the front page, I just change my hairstyle."**
>
> —HILLARY CLINTON

DID YOU KNOW . . . ?

- Clinton was the first "baby boomer" president from the generation born after World War II.
- The Clinton-Gore administration put up the first White House Web page.
- Socks the cat and Buddy the chocolate lab lived with the Clintons at the White House.
- Clinton collects saxophones, both miniature and life-sized.

Buddy and Bill.

Socks at a press conference.

THE CLINTON FAMILY

Father William Jefferson Blythe III (1918–1946)
Occupation Salesman
Stepfather Roger Clinton (1909–1967)
Occupation Car salesman
Mother Virginia Dell Cassidy Blythe Clinton Dwire Kelley
Occupation Nurse
Wife Hillary Diane Rodham Clinton
Birth October 26, 1947, Chicago, Illinois
Occupation Lawyer; senator
Marriage October 11, 1975
Children Chelsea Victoria (b. 1980)

Chelsea, Hillary, and Bill Clinton celebrate at a 1996 inaugural ball.

Timeline of the Clinton Presidency

US Events	World Events
1993 World Trade Center bombed	
	1994 English Channel Tunnel opens
1994 O. J. Simpson arrested	
	1995 Gas attack in Tokyo subway
1995 Oklahoma City bombing	
	1995 Israel's prime minister Yitzhak Rabin assassinated
	1996 Mad cow disease hits Britain
	1997 Hale-Bopp Comet visible
1997 NASA receives first Mars images	
	1997 Princess Diana dies in crash
	1997 Scientists clone sheep
1997 Tiger Woods wins Masters	
	1999 Euro is currency of Europe
1999 JFK Jr. dies in plane accident	
1999 Columbine High School shootings	
	2000 Millennium celebrated worldwide

George W. Bush

"Dubya"

2001–2009

After winning the presidency in a hotly contested election, George W. Bush went on to receive high approval ratings for his handling of post–9/11 America. His involvement in a controversial war with Iraq, however, left the country with a staggering deficit and tarnished his earlier popularity.

Bush was born in Connecticut but grew up in the Texas oil country. After completing his education in New England, he returned to Texas to begin a career in the energy industry. He also actively supported his father's 1988 presidential campaign. In 1989 Bush and several other businessmen bought the Texas Rangers baseball franchise, which raised his profile in the state. He was elected governor in 1975, running as a "compassionate conservative."

With his campaign platform of "a return to family values," Bush beat Al Gore in 2000's close presidential race. During his first term Bush reformed the country's education system with the No Child Left Behind Act. In addition to modernizing Medicare, including the first prescription drug benefit for seniors, he also signed significant tax relief bills for workers and investors. He did not accept global warming as a reality, however, and his refusal to sign the Kyoto Protocol to control climate change angered environmentalists.

The Darkest Morning

When Arab terrorists attacked multiple American targets on the morning of September 11, 2001, and destroyed the World Trade Center, President Bush responded by creating the Department of Homeland Security. States received funding for attack preparedness and airport security was improved. In this "War on Terror," the Patriot Act passed, which approved phone taps and Internet surveillance and allowed law enforcement officials to detain suspected terrorists.

"Freedom itself was attacked this morning by a faceless coward."

Bush's determination to seek out the Islamic radicals behind the attacks led to the US bombing of terrorist stronghold Afghanistan. Bush also ordered the invasion of Iraq. Although reports at the time claimed that the Iraqis had weapons of mass destruction, these reports eventually proved false.

Bush won a second term in 2004, but his luster had started to fade, even among Republicans. His harsh stand on illegal immigrants drew fire from moderates, and his delayed response to the devastation of Hurricane Katrina stunned the Gulf Coast states. Many Americans also questioned the continued involvement in a war that was growing increasingly expensive and had caused America to lose its "peacekeeper" status in the eyes of the world.

Bush left office with many new safeguards in place for national security, but the country was facing a recession, fuel prices were skyrocketing, and the resolution of the Iraq war was still uncertain.

BIOGRAPHICAL FACTS

Birth July 6, 1946, New Haven, Connecticut

Religion Methodist

Education Yale University (graduated 1968); Harvard Business School (graduated 1975)

Occupation Businessman; baseball team owner

Other Offices Governor of Texas

Military Service Fighter pilot, Texas Air National Guard

Political Party Republican

Vice President Richard Cheney

Age at Inauguration 54

George W., age nine, on a visit to one of his father's Texas oil fields.

Laura Bush. The former librarian committed herself to the causes of literacy and women's health.

> "We can overcome evil with greater good."
>
> —Laura Bush

DID YOU KNOW...?

Miss Beazley gives Willie a kiss for Valentine's Day, while Barney (left) looks on.

- The Bush pets include two Scottish terriers, Barney and Miss Beazley, and a cat, Willie.
- In 2001 former librarian First Lady Laura Bush launched the first National Book Festival.
- The Bush daughters, Barbara and Jenna, are fraternal twins.
- Bush's younger brother Jeb served as the governor of Florida.

THE BUSH FAMILY

Father George Herbert Walker Bush (b. 1924)

Occupation Oil industry; public servant; president

Mother Barbara Pierce Bush (b. 1925)

Wife Laura Welch Bush (b. 1946)

Birth November 4, 1946, Midland, Texas

Occupation Teacher; librarian

Marriage November 5, 1977

Children Barbara Pierce (b. 1981), Jenna Welch (b. 1981)

The first lady and the president and their daughters, fraternal twins Barbara and Jenna.

Timeline of the Bush Presidency

US Events	World Events
2001 9/11 terrorist attacks	
2003 Space shuttle *Columbia* disaster	
	2003 French heat wave kills 15,000
2003 The Northeast Blackout	
	2003 Iran earthquake kills 28,000
	2004 Indian Ocean tsunami
	2005 London and Madrid bombings
	2005 The *Huygens* probe lands on Saturn's moon Titan
2005 Steve Chen, Chad Hurley, and Jawed Karim launch YouTube	
	2005 Kashmir earthquake kills 80,000
	2005 Pope Benedict XVI elected
2005 Hurricane Katrina hits Gulf Coast	
	2007 Former Iraqi dictator Saddam Hussein hanged
	2007 World population is 6.6 billion
2007 Virginia Tech shootings	
	2008 Benazir Bhutto, first woman ever elected prime minister of an Islamic state, is assassinated

The Election Process

Ronald Reagan gives his acceptance speech at the 1988 Republican National Convention.

The Constitution provides for a presidential election every four years, which is held on the first Tuesday of November. But many months before this date, hopeful candidates begin raising money for their campaigns. Each political party, meanwhile, chooses a city for its convention, where the candidate will actually receive the formal nomination. Even if a sitting president is running unopposed, the party still holds a nominating convention, in part because the festive atmosphere creates a buzz of enthusiasm for the candidate.

The statewide elections, called primaries and caucuses, lead up to the convention. These begin in January and run throughout the spring. The winning candidates receive a certain number of delegates from each state, who will then attend the convention and vote for them. The democratic Party, unlike the Republicans, also provides for a large number of unpledged "superdelegates" at the convention: elected officeholders and party officials who can tip the voting toward their favorite candidate.

Once the candidates have been nominated by their party, they choose a vice presidential running mate, usually someone who will balance the ticket geographically. If there has been discord within a party during the primaries, it usually evaporates as parties unify behind their chosen candidate.

Making a Critical Decision

VOTE

How voters view a candidate is often affected by the news media, polls, and advertising. Debates between candidates are televised so that voters can hear them speak on issues such as the economy, foreign policy, education, and tax programs. Physical appearance can also play a large part in a candidate's appeal. Although gender or race can sway voters, it's not a given. In the Democratic primaries of 2008, many women supported Barack Obama, while many blacks voted for Hillary Clinton. Ultimately, a voter should make a choice based on the candidates' stand on the issues—called their "platform"—and their experience and values.

Campaign banner for the Lincoln/Hamlin ticket during the 1880 presidential election.

"I go by the great republican principle, that the people will have the virtue and intelligence to select men of virtue and intelligence."

—James Madison

The Campaign Trail

Once the candidates have been nominated, campaigning is stepped up. The presidential aspirants travel throughout the country giving speeches, attending fund-raising dinners, making public appearances, and sitting in on televised "town meetings." Meanwhile their party supporters are busy drumming up votes: organizing national advertising campaigns, making phone calls, sending out direct-mail flyers, and distributing lawn signs and bumper stickers.

THE ELECTORAL COLLEGE

On Election Day, every registered citizen age 18 and over has the right to vote. Yet unlike some republics with high attendance at the polls, America's voter turnout is often less than 60 percent. One possible cause for this may be that the popular vote does not determine who becomes president. This falls to a system the founders called the College of Electors.

The Electoral College works in a somewhat complicated way. After an election, a block of electors is selected based on the popular vote in each state. The number of electors matches a state's number of congressional representatives. These electors are pledged to vote for a specific presidential and vice presidential candidate when they convene at their state capitols in December. Legally, however, the electors are not bound to vote for their "pledged" candidate. If they vote differently they are called "unfaithful" or "faithless" electors. Their votes are sent to the president of the Senate, who counts them. An absolute majority is necessary to win: with 538 electors in total, the winner must receive 270 votes.

If no candidate receives a majority, it rests with the House of Representatives to determine the next president. Each state gets one vote, and, again, a majority must be achieved. Thomas Jefferson and John Quincy Adams were both elected by the House when the Electoral College could not reach a majority.

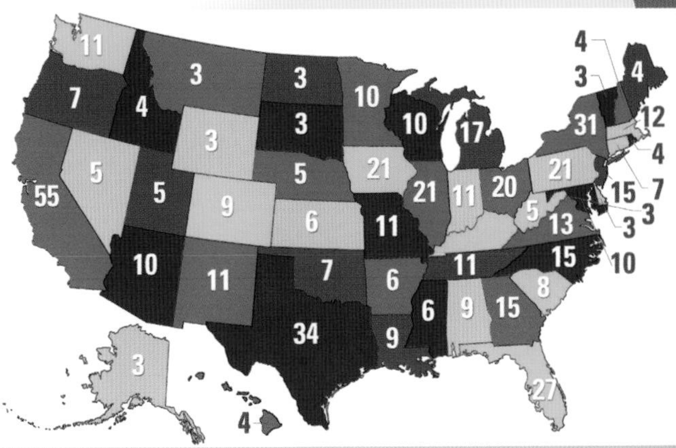

Number of electoral votes by state, as of 2000

THE PARTY SYSTEM

Currently the two major parties in the United States are the Democrats and the Republicans, but there have also been candidates from other parties, such as the Libertarians. Independent candidates, with no party allegiance, must get a large number of signatures to support their nominations, and they must file certificates of candidacy.

Political party symbols: Above, the Democratic donkey; left, the Republican elephant.

The Right to Vote

The US Constitution does not explicitly state a "right to vote," and throughout American history the issue of just who can vote, and who cannot, has raised debate. Today both federal and state laws determine eligibility, but although each state ultimately decides which citizens it allows to vote, amendments to the Constitution have imposed some national standards on voting laws. Since the Civil War 15 voting amendments passed, and five of them extended the right to important groups once excluded from the election process:

15th Amendment **(1870)**

No law may restrict any race from voting.

19th Amendment **(1920)**

No law may restrict any sex from voting.

24th Amendment **(1964)**

No law can condition the right to vote in federal elections on payment of a poll tax or other type of tax.

26th Amendment **(1971)**

No law may restrict those 18 years of age or older from voting because of their age.

Women suffragists riot at a polling place in 1908. In the United States, women did not receive the right to vote until 1920.

Barack Obama

"The Torchbearer" **2009–**

When young Illinois legislator Barack Obama delivered the keynote address at the 2004 Democratic National Convention, it was clear that a powerful new voice had arisen in the party. He was elected to the US Senate that same year, and four years later found himself on the road to the Oval Office as America's first minority president.

Obama was the child of an American mother and a Kenyan father. His parents met while at the University of Hawaii, but they separated when he was two years old. His mother remarried an Indonesian, and the family moved to Jakarta, where Obama lived until he was ten. He then returned to Hawaii to live with his mother's parents until he graduated from high school in Honolulu.

He attended Columbia University, majoring in political science, and after spending several years as a community organizer in Chicago, he entered Harvard Law School. While working as a summer associate at the Chicago law firm of Sidley & Austin, he met future wife Michelle Robinson. The couple married in 1992.

Obama served seven years in the Illinois Senate before gaining a seat in the US Senate in 2004. He quickly put together a team of experienced advisors to coach him on a wide range of issues. As senator he worked to eliminate voter fraud, outlaw the use of anti-personnel mines, and restrict greenhouse gases. As a member of the Senate Foreign Relations Committee, he visited Eastern Europe, the Middle East, Africa, Russia, and Ukraine.

Time for Change

Obama's bid for president attracted a varied segment of the population. His campaign slogan, "Change We Can Believe In," promised to shake up the old-boy network in Washington by providing fresh ideas and legislative reforms. But first Obama had to cope with the issue of his "Muslim" family connections. He assured the press that neither his father nor stepfather held radical religious beliefs. Yet he himself was impressed by the role the religious community played in supporting minority rights, and in 1988 he joined Chicago's "megachurch," Trinity United Church of Christ.

"I wouldn't be here if, time and again, the torch had not been passed to a new generation."

After a neck-and-neck race with Hillary Clinton during the Democratic primaries, Obama received his party's nomination. In the 2008 election he beat Republican John McCain. Obama then began the hard work of fulfilling his campaign promises of withdrawing US troops from Iraq, keeping Social Security and Medicare solvent, combating climate change, and implementing universal health care. He is currently serving a second term, having beaten Mitt Romney in the 2012 election.

BIOGRAPHICAL FACTS

Birth August 4, 1961, Honolulu, Hawaii
Religion United Church of Christ
Education Columbia University (graduated 1983); Harvard Law School (graduated 1991)
Occupation Lawyer
Other Offices US senator
Political Party Democratic
Vice President Joseph R. Biden, Jr.
Age at Inauguration 48

"Barack didn't pledge riches. Only a life that would be interesting. On that promise he's delivered."
—Michelle Obama

The first lady comes to her position with an impressive résumé: she graduated Harvard Law in 1989, was associate dean at the University of Chicago, and was a member of six boards of directors.

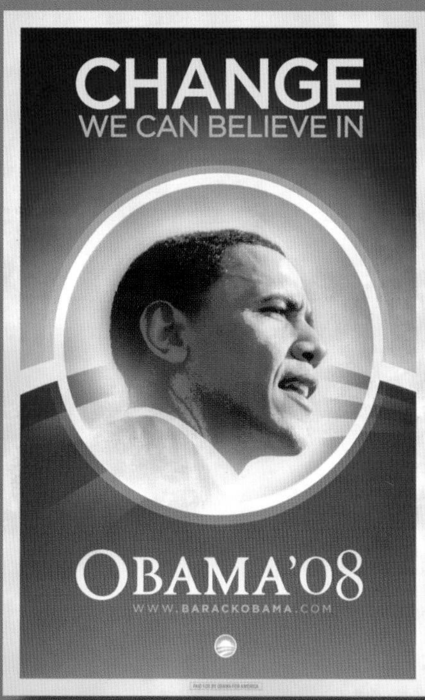

DID YOU KNOW . . . ?

- Obama was the first African American president of the Harvard Law Review.
- Obama was a member of his high school basketball team and still enjoys the game.
- The audio version of Obama's first book, *Dreams from My Father*, received a Grammy nomination.
- Obama's second book, *The Audacity of Hope*, became a *New York Times* best-seller and earned him a Grammy for the audio version.

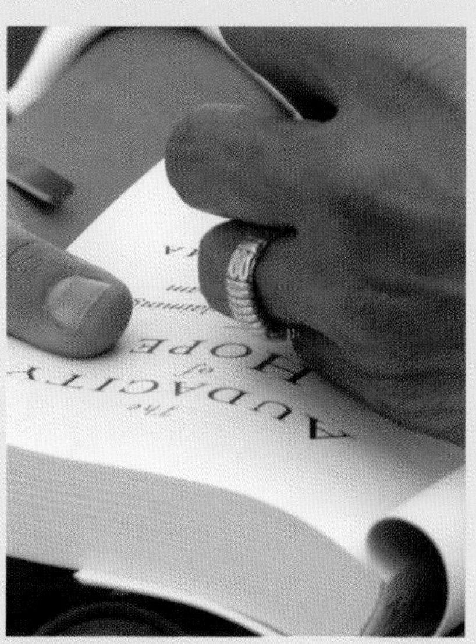

Obama autographs a copy of *The Audacity of Hope* for a supporter while campaigning.

THE OBAMA FAMILY

Father Barack Obama Sr. (1936–1982)
Occupation Economist
Mother Stanley Ann Dunham Soetoro (1942–1995)
Occupation Anthropologist
Wife Michelle LaVaughn Robinson Obama
Birth January 17, 1964, Chicago, Illinois
Occupation Lawyer; vice president for community and external affairs at University of Chicago Hospitals
Marriage October 18, 1992
Children Malia Ann (b. 1998); Natasha "Sasha" (b. 2001)

The Obama family: Michelle and Barack with daughters, Sasha (on her mother's lap) and Malia.

"A man of relative youth yet maturity, a wise observer of the human condition."
—Gary Hart

Find Out More

Presidents helped to shape the eras in which they served. If you'd like to understand how people lived during those times or want to learn more about the history of the country, here are some books and movies that will give you a window into the past.

The Founding Presidents

The 4th of July Story by Alice Dalgliesh

The Declaration of Independence by Dennis B. Fradin

The Constitution by Warren Colman

If You Were There When They Signed the Constitution by Elizabeth Levy

1776 (DVD, 1972) starring Williams Daniels,

If You Lived in Colonial Times by Ann McGovern

Johnny Tremain by Esther Forbes

A Flag for Our Country by Eve Spencer

George Washington by Cheryl Harness

George Washington (DVD, 1995) starring Barry Bostwick

The Amazing Life of Benjamin Franklin by James Cross Giblin

America's Paul Revere by Esther Forbes

George vs. George: The Revolutionary War as Seen by Both Sides by Rosalyn Schanzer

The Revolutionary John Adams by Cheryl Harness

John Adams (DVD, 2008) starring Paul Giamatti

Thomas Jefferson by Cheryl Harness

James Madison and Dolley Madison and Their Times by Robert Quackenbush

Amos Fortune: Free Man by Elizabeth Yates

The Sign of the Beaver by Elizabeth George Speare

Presidents of an Expanding Nation

The Cabin Faced West by Jean Fritz

The Ghosts of Stony Clove by Eileen Charbonneau

Danger Along the Ohio by Patricia Willis

Caddie Woodlawn by Carol Ryrie Brink

A Gathering of Days: A New England Girl's Journal, 1830–1832 by Joan W. Blos

Timmy O'Dowd and the Big Ditch: A Story of the Glory Days on the Old Erie Canal by Len Hilts

The Incredible Journey of Lewis and Clark by Rhoda Blumberg

Streams to the River, River to the Sea by Scott O'Dell

A Line in the Sand: The Alamo Diary of Lucinda Lawrence, Gonzales, Texas, 1836 by Sherry Garland

The Alamo (DVD, 2004) starring Billy Bob Thornton

Night of the Cruel Moon by Stanley Hoig

Presidents of a Nation in Conflict

Abe Lincoln Grows Up by Carl Sandburg

Lincoln: A Photobiography by Russell Freedman

Across Five Aprils by Irene Hunt

Behind Rebel Lines: The Incredible Story of Emma Edmonds, Civil War Spy by Seymour Reit

Glory (DVD, 1989) starring Denzel Washington

The Perilous Road by William O. Steele

Friendly Persuasion by Jessamyn West

Friendly Persuasion (DVD, 1956) starring Gary Cooper

The Red Badge of Courage by Stephen Crane

Gettysburg (DVD, 1993) starring Jeff Daniels

Shades of Gray by Carolyn Reader

Christmas in the Big House: Christmas in the Quarters by Patricia C. McKissack

Freedom Train: The Story of Harriet Tubman by Dorothy Sterling

Prudence Crandall: Woman of Courage by Elizabeth Yates

Sing Down the Moon by Scott O'Dell

The Slave Dancer by Paula Fox

Lyddie by Katherine Paterson

Gold Fever by Verla Kay

Presidents of the Gilded Age

Gilded Age and Progressive Era by Rebecca Valentine

Paperboy by Isabelle Holland

Little Britches: Father and I Were Ranchers by Ralph Moody

How the West Was Won (DVD, 1972) starring James Stewart

The *Little House* books by Laura Ingalls Wilder

Sarah, Plain and Tall by Patricia MacLachlan

Sarah, Plain and Tall (DVD, 1999) starring Glenn Close

Out of the Dust by Karen Hesse

Presidents of an Emerging Power

Theodore Roosevelt, Fighting Patriot by Clara Ingram Judson

Portrait of the Panama Canal by William Friar

The Wright Brothers: How They Invented the Airplane by Russell Freedman

Strawberry Girl by Lois Lenski

When Jessie Came Across the Sea by Amy Hest

Streets of Gold by Rosemary Wells

All-of-a-Kind Family by Sydney Talor

Sergeant York and the Great War by Alvin C. York, ed. Richard "Little Bear" Wheeler

Sergeant York (DVD, 1941) starring Gary Cooper

The Hindenburg by Patrick O'Brien

To Kill a Mockingbird by Harper Lee

We Want Jobs!: A Story of the Great Depression by Robert J. Norrell

Eleanor Roosevelt: A Life of Discovery by Russell Freedman

Sunrise at Campobello, VHS, 1960, starring Ralph Bellamy

Sounder (VHS, 1972) starring Cicely Tyson

Anne Frank: The Diary of a Young Girl by Anne Frank

The Diary of Anne Frank (DVD, 2001) starring Hannah Taylor Gordon

The Good Fight: How World War II Was Won by Stephen E. Ambrose

Key Battles of World War II (20th Century Perspectives) by Fiona Reynoldson

A Boy at War: A Novel of Pearl Harbor by Harry Mazer

Sadako and the Thousand Paper Cranes by Eleanor Coerr

Number the Stars by Lois Lowry

Roll of Thunder, Hear My Cry by Mildred D. Taylor

The Freedom Rides: Journey for Justice by James Haskins

The Voice that Challenged a Nation: Marian Anderson and the Struggle for Equal Rights by Russell Freedman

Ashes of Roses by Mary Jane Auch

Navajo Code Talkers by Nathan Aaseng

PT 109: John F. Kennedy in World War II by Robert J. Donovan and Robert Donovan

PT 109 (VHS, 1963) starring Cliff Robertson

Cold War Presidents

Peacebound Trains by Haemi Balgassi

Superpower Rivalry: The Cold War, 1945-1991 by Tony McAleavy

The Cold War Pigeon Patrols: And Other Animal Spies by Danielle Denega

Truman (DVD, 2000) starring Gary Sinese

Profiles in Courage by John F. Kennedy

The Cuban Missile Crisis: The Cold War Goes Hot by Jim Whiting

Thirteen Days (DVD, 2001) starring Kevin Costner

The 1960s: Arts and Entertainment by Stuart Kallen

Goodbye, Vietnam by Gloria Whelan

The History of NASA by Ray Spangenburg and Kit Moser

Apollo 13 (DVD, 1995) starring Tom Hanks

Presidents in a Global Economy

Understanding September 11th by Mitch Frank

The War In Iraq by David Downing

An Inconvenient Truth (DVD, 2006) produced by Al Gore

The Audacity of Hope by Barack Obama

Fahrenheit 9/11 (DVD, 2004) directed by Michael Moore

Index

Acknowledgments & Credits

The author wishes to thank her parents, John and Doris—running mates for more than five decades.

And Lisa Purcell, that rare combination of editor *and* designer.

CREDITS

DDEPL = *Dwight D. Eisenhower Presidential Library*; FDRPL = *Franklin D. Roosevelt Presidential Library and Museum*; GBPL = *George Bush Presidential Library and Museum*; GRFPL = *Gerald R. Ford Presidential Library and Museum*; JFKPL = *John F. Kennedy Presidential Library and Museum*; JI = *Jupiter Images*; HSTL = *Harry S. Truman Library and Museum*; LBJPL = *Lyndon Baines Johnson Presidential Library and Museum*; LoC = *Library of Congress*; PD = *public domain*; RRPL = *Ronald Reagan Presidential Foundation and Library;* SS = *Shutterstock*; Wiki = *Wikipedia*; WJCPL = *William J. Clinton Presidential Library*

l = left; *r* = right; *t* = top; *b* = bottom; *c* =center

Background photo on pages 3, 4–5, 6–7, 8–9, 16–17, 24–35, 30–31, 38–39, 46–47, 58–59, 62–63, 70–71, 78–79, 82–83, 90–91, 104–105, 116–117, 124–125, 134–135 by Jason Stitt/SS

Table of Contents

4*bl* LoC **4***tr* LoC **5***tl* DDEPL **5***bl* LoC **5***cr* barackobama.com **6** Wiki **7***bl* U.S. Air Force **7***tr* GRFPL

The Founding Presidents

8–9 U.S. Senate **10** Rembrandt Peale/PD **11***tr* LoC **11***c* Scott Catron/Wiki **11***bl* LoC **12***tl* Rudi Von Briel/IndexOpen **12***tr* John Trumbull/PD **12***bc* LoC **12***br* Wiki **13***t* LoC **13***b* Joseph Desire Court/PD **14** John Trumbull/PD **15***cl* New York Public Library **15***br* LoC **16** LoC **17***tl* LoC **17***cr* JFKPL **17***cr* JFKPL **17***bl* LoC **18** LoC **19***tc* David Ball/Wiki **19***cl* Wiki **19***bc* PD **19***br* LoC **20***tl* LoC **20***br* LoC **21***t* Matt Kozlowski/Wiki **21**c 7716430100/SS **21**b LoC **22** LoC **23***cl* LoC **23***br* Gilbert Stuart/PD

Presidents of an Expanding Nation

24–25 LoC **26** Willian James Hubbard/ PD **27***tr* SS/Victorian Traditions **27***cl* Lisa Purcell **27***br* LoC **28** LoC **29** Charles Bird King/PD **30***br* LoC **30***tr* LoC **30***bc* LoC **31** LoC **32** LoC **33***tr* LoC **33***cl* LoC **34** Wiki **35***tr* LoC **35***bl* LoC **36** LoC **37***tr* LoC **37***cl* LoC **37***b* LoC

Presidents of a Nation in Conflict

38–39 LoC **40** LoC **41***tr* U.S. Marine Corp **41***bc* JI **42** LoC **43***tr* LoC **43***cl* James K. Polk Memorial Association **44** James Reid Lambdin/PD **45***tr* LoC **45***cl* LoC **45***br* LoC **46** JI **47***bl* U.S. Senate **47***tr* Diliff/Wiki **48** LoC **49***tr* LoC **49***cl* LoC **49***br* Millard Fillmore House **50** George Healy/PD **51***tr* LoC **51***cl* U.S. Senate **51***br* LoC **52** LoC **53***tr* LoC **53***cl* LoC **53***bl* LoC **54** Wiki **55***tr* LoC **55***cl* LoC **55***bl* LoC **56***tl* LoC **56***tr* LoC **56***br* JI **56***bc* Wiki **57***tl* LoC **57***cr* Wiki **57***br* LoC **58***cl* LoC **58***tr* LoC **58***br* LoC **59***tl* JFKPL **59***tr* LoC **60** LoC **61***tr* Andrew Jackson National Historic Site **61***cl* LoC **61***bc* LoC

Presidents of the Gilded Age

62–63 LoC **64** LoC **65***tr* LoC **65***cl* LoC **65***br* LoC **66** LoC **67***tr* LoC **67***cl* LoC **67***bc* Rutherford B. Hayes Presidential Center **68** LoC **69***cl* LoC **69***br* LoC **70***tc* LoC **70***bl* LoC **71***tr* GRFPL **71***cr* LoC **72** LoC **73***tr* LoC **73***cl* LoC **73***br* LoC **74** Wiki **75***tr* LoC **75***cl* Wiki **75***bc* LoC **76** LoC **77***cl* LoC **77***tr* LoC **77**b LoC **78***bl* James K. Polk Memorial Association **78***tr* RRPL **78***br* Department of State **79** Department of Education **80** LoC **81***tr* LoC **81***cl* LoC **81***br* LoC

Presidents of an Emerging Power

82–83 LoC **84** LoC **85***tc* LoC **85***cl* Waugsberg/Wiki **85***tr* LoC **85***br* LoC **86***tl* LoC **86***tr* LoC **86**c LoC **86***bl* LoC **86***bc* LoC **86***br* LoC **87***cl* U.S. Navy **87***tr* LoC **87***bc* LoC **88** LoC **89***tr* LoC **89***cl* LoC **89***bc* LoC **90***tl* Gary Blakeley/SS **90***bl* LoC **90***br* LoC **91***tl* LoC **91***tr* LoC **91***cr* Department of Justice **92** LoC **93***tr* LoC **93***cl* LoC **93***cr* LoC **93***bc* LoC **94** LoC **95***tr* LoC **95***cl* LoC **95***br* LoC **96** LoC **97***tr* LoC **97***cl* LoC **97***br* LoC **98** LoC **99**trLoC **99***cl* LoC **99***br* LoC **100** LoC **101***tc* LoC **101***tr* FDRPL **101***cl* FDRPL **101***bc* FDRPL **101***br* Wiki **102***cl* Ritu Jethan/Big Stock Photos **102***tr* LoC **102***bl* FDRPL **102***br* FDRPL **103***tr* FDRPL **103***cl* FDRPL **103***br* FDRPL

Cold War Presidents

104–105 LoC **106** HS*Tl* **107***tr* HS*Tl* **107***cl* HS*Tl* **107***cr* HS*Tl* **107***br* HS*Tl* **108** DDEPL **109***tr* DDEPL **109***cl* DDEPL **109***cr* Lisa Purcell **109***c* PD **109***br* DDEPL **110** JFKPL **111***tc* JFKPL **111***tr* LoC **111**c JFKPL **111***bl* JFKPL **111***br* JFKPL **112***cl* JFKPL **112***bl* LoC **112***tc* NASA **112***cr* NASA/Kennedy Space Center **112***cr* Wiki **113***tc* Wiki **113***tr* JFKPL **113***tl* JFKPL **113***cl* JFKPL **113***br* JFKPL **114** PD/National Portrait Gallery **115***tr* LBJPL **115***cl* LBJPL **115***cl* LBJPL **115***c* LBJPL **115***cr* LBJPL **115***br* LBJPL **116***tr* GBPL **116***cl* PD/National Portrait Gallery **116***bl* LoC **116**c LoC **116***bc* National First Ladies' Library **117***tl* Wiki **117***cl* LoC **117***tl* (box) LoC **117***cl* (box) LoC **117***bl* (box) LoC **117***tr* (box) DDEPL **117***cr* (box) LoC **117***br* (box)Veni Markovski/Wiki **117***br* LoC **118** RNLBF **119***tr* RNLBF **119***cl* LoC **119***c* RNLBF **119***br* RNLBF **119***cr* RNLBF **120** GRFPL **121***tc* GRFPL **121***tr* GRFPL **121***cl* GRFPL **121***bl* GRFPL **121***br* GRFPL **122** LoC **123***tl* LoC **123***cl* Suzanne Tucker/SS **123***cr* LoC **123***bc* Jimmy Carter Presidential Library and Museum

Presidents in a Global Economy

124–125 Jonathan Green/SS **126** RRPL **127***tl* RRPL **127***cl* RRPL **127***cr* RRPL **127***br* RRPL **128** PD/National Portrait Gallery **129***tr* GBPL **129***cl* GBPL **129**c GBPL **129***cr* GBPL **129***bl* GBPL **130** WJCPL **131***tr* WJCPL **131***cl* WJCPL **131***cr* WJCPL **131***cr* WJCPL **131***br* WJCPL **132** White House **133***tr* GBPL **133***cr* GBPL **133***cl* White House **133***br* GBPL **134***tl* RRPL **134***bc* LoC **134***tr* Jacob/SS **135***tr* Wiki **135***cl* Jacob/SS **135***bl* Jacob/SS **135***br* JI **136** barackobama.com **137***tr* barackobama.com **137***cl* barackobama.com **137***cr* barakobama.com **137***bc* barackobama.com

DATE DUE

PRINTED IN U.S.A.